T0295521

The China–US Trade War

An unprecedented trade war broke out between the world's two largest economies in 2018 and escalated subsequently. It is the first major economic conflict to occur in the era of globalization, with its aftermath going far beyond trade. The trade war weighs heavily on China and the United States and threatens the world economy and the global trading system.

This book provides a timely account of the China–US trade war with insights into its causes and consequences. Examining through the lenses of both history and theory, it analyzes the context and causes of the trade war, the intertwined processes of tariff combat and trade negotiations, and the impacts on international trade, foreign direct investment, macroeconomic performance and firm behaviour. It also addresses the long-term strategic and geopolitical implications of the ongoing trade and economic confrontation.

This book will appeal to those interested in international economics and politics, global governance and development.

Guoyong Liang is a senior economist at the United Nations Conference on Trade and Development. He holds a Ph.D. from the Rotterdam School of Management, Erasmus University. Dr. Liang has published widely, playing an important role in public policy debates on international economic issues.

Haoyuan Ding is Associate Professor and Assistant Dean of the College of Business at Shanghai University of Finance and Economics. He holds a Ph.D. from the Chinese University of Hong Kong. His research interests include international economics, development economics and the Chinese economy.

Routledge Focus on Economics and Finance

The fields of economics are constantly expanding and evolving. This growth presents challenges for readers trying to keep up with the latest important insights. Routledge Focus on Economics and Finance presents short books on the latest big topics, linking in with the most cutting-edge economics research.

Individually, each title in the series provides coverage of a key academic topic, whilst collectively the series forms a comprehensive collection across the whole spectrum of economics.

Automation, Capitalism and the End of the Middle Class
Jon-Arild Johannessen

Cryptocurrencies
A Primer on Digital Money
Mark Grabowski

Knowledge Infrastructure and Higher Education in India
Kaushalesh Lal and Shampa Paul

What Drives China's Economy
Economic, Socio-Political, Historical and Cultural Factors
Qing-Ping Ma

Environmentally Sustainable Industrial Development in China
Yanqing Jiang and Xu Yuan

The China–US Trade War
Guoyong Liang and Haoyuan Ding

For more information about this series, please visit: www.routledge.com/Routledge-Focus-on-Economics-and-Finance/book-series/RFEF

The China–US Trade War

Guoyong Liang and Haoyuan Ding

Routledge
Taylor & Francis Group

LONDON AND NEW YORK

First published 2021
by Routledge
2 Park Square, Milton Park, Abingdon, Oxon OX14 4RN

and by Routledge
52 Vanderbilt Avenue, New York, NY 10017

Routledge is an imprint of the Taylor & Francis Group, an informa business

British Library Cataloguing in Publication Data
A catalogue record for this book is available from the British Library

Library of Congress Cataloging in Publication Data
Names: Liang, Guoyong, author. | Ding, Haoyuan, author.
Title: The China–US trade war / Guoyong Liang and Haoyuan Ding.
Description: Abingdon, Oxon ; New York, NY : Routledge, [2021] | Series:
  Routledge focus on economic & finance | Includes bibliographical
  references and index.
Identifiers: LCCN 2020012602 (print) | LCCN 2020012603 (ebook)
Subjects: LCSH: United States—Commerce—China. | China—Commerce—
  United States. | United States—Foreign economic relations—China. |
  China—Foreign economic relations—United States. | Tariff—United
  States. | Tariff—China.
Classification: LCC HF3128 .L53 2021 (print) | LCC HF3128 (ebook) |
  DDC 382.0951073—dc23
LC record available at https://lccn.loc.gov/2020012602
LC ebook record available at https://lccn.loc.gov/2020012603

ISBN: 978-0-367-36314-7 (hbk)
ISBN: 978-0-429-34524-1 (ebk)

Typeset in Times New Roman
by Apex CoVantage, LLC

To our parents

Contents

Introduction

In May 2018, we published a column in FTChinese.com titled "Four Key Dimensions of the Upcoming China-US Trade War", the first of a series on this issue. Here are some excerpts:

> Trade war may bring unpredictable risks to both economies. More importantly, we should not only look at trade issues, economic figures and static effects, but also consider indirect impacts, political implications and long-term consequences. . . . In the face of heated discussions about the trade war, the author has always stressed that peaceful China-US trade and economic cooperation is of paramount importance. A trade war is both losing and hurting. Facing the threat of tariffs, countries should "prepared to fight" tactically, but emphasize "prevent the war" strategically. As long as they insist on negotiations and reach a compromise, both sides will win.

Similarly, at a seminar in Shanghai in April 2017, we argued that the "100-Day Plan" – a trade talk agreed by presidents of China and the United States – would offer a fleeting window of opportunity for the two countries to strike a deal on trade. Despite these and other precautions, an unprecedented trade war broke out in July 2018 and subsequently escalated. It has significantly affected the world's two largest economies, threatened the global trading system and has become a major risk for the world economy. Furthermore, it has reshaped the China–US relationship, demonstrating far-reaching political and geopolitical implications in the long run. From a historical perspective, the China–US trade war is the first major economic conflict that has occurred in the era of globalization, with its aftermath going far beyond trade. In terms of scope and scale, the amount of affected trade flows has gone from billions of dollars, the earlier record level in history, up to hundreds of billions of dollars, with thousands of products targeted.

In this book, we would like to provide an informative account of the China–US trade war, an insightful explanation of its causes, and an in-depth assessment of its impacts. We aim to deal with this crucial topic in a timely and comprehensive manner, combining reliable "storytelling", rigorous analyses and a reader-friendly way of presentation. Up till now, studies on the China–US trade war have been focused on specific aspects, and comprehensive analysis is missing. This book attempts to fill the gap. It provides the fullest and most engaging account available of the China–US trade war as of early 2020. In this "handbook" on this historic event, readers can find various useful information – its causes, combating and negotiating processes, and consequences. More importantly, the book sheds light on our theoretical understanding of economic conflicts in general and trade wars in particular.

The research target of the book is a very recent phenomenon, which has been rapidly unfolding and constantly evolving. The analysis covers up to the signing of the Phase One trade agreement on 15 January 2020, which is a milestone and turning point of the ongoing trade war, and its coming into effect one month later. In the meantime, our research target has become increasingly complicated and, thus, the authors face various challenges: How to collect timely, reliable and useful data for our empirical studies of this unprecedented trade war; how to gather, analyze and present data in an objective manner; how to overcome the theoretical difficulties related to complexity and complication of the phenomenon, and examine it scientifically from different angles and at different levels; how to have an overall grasp of the issue, combining economic, political, geopolitical and historical perspectives, while looking through different lenses of trade, investment, technology and finance.

A sound approach to data collection, careful methodological considerations and an interdisciplinary theoretical underpinning are crucial for overcoming these challenges. In addition, we need a well-designed analytical framework, which can help us answer questions about why the trade war is happening, how it is evolving and its impacts and implications. This framework integrates the international-, national- and industrial-levels of analyses and incorporates the short-, medium- and long-term time dimensions. Though political and economic contexts are different, it should be able to apply to the analysis of economic trade conflicts at large, including the ongoing tension between China and the United States.

The causes of a trade war are diversified, ranging from economic to political, national to international, and direct to indirect factors. A conflict at the international level may be closely related to the structural features of the two involved economies at the national level. As a radical and unconventional way of solving disputes, a trade war is directly related to bilateral trade and economic issues, but may be indirectly related to complicated political processes and a broader geopolitical context. Thus, for a better understanding of the causes of a trade war, we need to examine not only trade conflicts, but also their economic background; not only economic determinants, but also political drives; and not only the bilateral relationship, but also its global context.

Trade wars affect the economy through both exports (for exporting countries that suffer from special tariffs) and imports (for importing countries that impose special tariffs). The potential impacts cover all aspects of a country's economy via both direct and indirect channels – affecting both industries and financial markets, enterprises (exporters and importers) and consumers. They involve macro-, meso- (i.e. industry-, local-) and micro-level effects on the short-, medium- and long-terms. Therefore, an effective assessment of the economic impact of trade wars will inevitably face the challenge of a comprehensive theoretical understanding of the complex mechanisms, and a multi-level and multi-dimensional analytical framework is needed. This framework covers the effects of trade wars on macroeconomy, international economic exchanges, a range of industries and a large number of economic entities. Based on such a framework, we can examine relevant economic variables at different levels, exploring the channels through which trade wars influence these variables and the interrelationship between them.

It is important to distinguish between export and import directions. From the perspective of "export direction", the specific influences of a trade war depend on how tariffs imposed on a country affect microeconomic entities, including enterprises that are directly affected by tariffs and other enterprises as well. The direct impact is first represented internationally, having negative diversion effects on exports and investment inflows. Thus, the trade war negatively affects production, employment and output in specific industries. At the macroeconomic level, trade wars directly affect economic growth through the changes in net exports and may indirectly affect capital formation and final consumption. From the perspective of "import direction", tariffs imposing on a foreign country could lead to an increase in the price of imported goods, which in turn affects consumer welfare, and could even affect the consumer price index at the macro level. The impacts of the "export direction" of one country and the "import direction" of another country are interrelated. From the perspective of political economic analysis, trade wars involve the distribution of welfare losses between the two countries, as well as the distribution of the negative impact of increased prices between importers and consumers.

The book has been prepared with all these theoretical and methodological considerations in mind. It is organized as follows.

Chapter 1 addresses several general issues related to trade wars, laying the foundation for the analysis of the China–US trade war in the subsequent chapters. It presents both historical and theoretical perspectives, covering not only the trade literature but also the game theoretical approach. Conventional trade theory, optimal tariff theory, strategic trade policy and cooperative and noncooperative policy, as well as the static and dynamic game theoretical tools, play an important role in deepening the understanding of trade war – its causes, consequences and processes. From two economies aiming at maximizing national welfare in pure trade theory, to two players engaging in strategic interaction in game theory, and then to different interest groups in two countries in political economics, the changes in assumptions and the expansion of analytical subjects bring the theory closer to reality.

Chapter 2 examines the background of the China–US trade war and analyzes the reasons of its outbreak. The relationship between American and Chinese economies is examined in the context of an evolving landscape of globalization, with the sustained interdependencies and unstainable imbalances between the economies explained. This relationship is also discussed in the context of the intensified rivalry between the United States, the world's only superpower after the end of the Cold War, and China, a "superpower" in the making after a sustained, spectacular ascent over four decades. A pivotal moment has come: the pre-existing mechanism for settling economic disputes between the two countries has become ineffective, leading to the emergence of a new one – not based on rules but on forces.

Chapter 3 examines the evolution of the China–US trade war, its initiation, escalation and ramification, the final results of which remains to be observed. The chapter also explores the associated trade negotiation, a complicated process of trade diplomacy that has led to the signing of an interim agreement. The agreement does not aim to promote free trade, but resorts to "managed trade". On the one hand, the theories reviewed in Chapter 1 will be applied to the specific case of the China–US trade war for exploring its tortuous processes, interactive characteristics and tit-for-tat confrontations. On the other hand, the study of this unique case and its comparison with other cases in history will help improve our theoretical understanding of trade wars in general.

Chapter 4 assesses the economic impacts of the China–US trade war. It covers economic variables at macro, meso and micro levels and analyzes from different dimensions, including international trade, foreign direct investment (FDI), economic growth, financial performance, business behaviour and the bilateral economic relationship at large. The chapter focuses on the two participating countries, but also addresses the implications of the China–US trade war from a global perspective and potential effects on third party countries, through for instance the channels of trade and invest-ment diversion. Although the Phase One agreement has been signed and the China–US negotiations have moved into a new stage, most special tar-iffs remain, particularly on Chinese exports. Their impacts will continue to unfold, the degree of which will affect the stances of the two countries during the following negotiations and therefore the final outcomes of the unprecedented trade war. The Phase Two negotiations will take a key step to end the trade war, the timing of which remains uncertain.

The effective analysis of the impact of the China–US trade war faces the practical problems of a short observation time and insufficient data, as well as the theoretical challenges of fully understanding its complex influenc-ing mechanism. For the observed dependent variables, there are various influencing factors, which are often interrelated. Thus, it requires a strong theoretical support and prudent methodological considerations in order to understand how and to what extent a trade war affects these economic vari-ables. Descriptive statistics are a crucial first step. Under the circumstance that econometric methods cannot be effectively applied, however, it is dif-ficult to quantify the impact of trade war and attribution is also a challenge. For the book as a whole, the availability of data limits the depth and breadth of its analysis.

In the game theoretical analysis of the trade war, we focus on trade and use the real export loss to calculate payoffs. Nevertheless, the real picture is much more complicated, as the two sides must consider many other fac-tors during the intertwined processes of trade war and trade negotiations. In the specific case of the China–US trade war, what is particularly important is the demand made by the United States to China during the trade talks, which started even before the first shot of the trade war. Unfortunately, both other factors and the US demand are not possible to be reflected in the game modelling. Therefore, cautions are needed for reaching a general conclu-sion based on such a modelling, and a more qualitative analysis is needed regarding the strategic dimension and interactive nature of the trade war.

Note

The views expressed in this book are those of the authors only and do not necessarily represent those of their affiliated organizations.

1 Trade wars

Review of history and theory

> Weapons are inauspicious instruments, not used by the gentleman.
>
> – Lao Tzu

Both historical and theoretical perspectives are needed to understand a trade war – its causes, processes and impacts – and to deal with it effectively. After a brief conceptual discussion, this chapter reviews history and theory about trade wars. The historical section of the chapter pays particular attention to the evolution of international trade policies and domestic trade politics of the United States, which have led to several major trade conflicts during the past century or so. The theoretical section of the chapter first provides a review of the existing literature in international economics, which helps us understand why trade wars break out and what their welfare effects are. It then presents the game theoretical approach, explaining how trade wars are fought and where they end.

1.1 The concept

"Trade wars" are international economic conflicts where two states use unusual restrictive measures to affect imports of goods or services from each other in order to achieve certain economic objectives. This definition distinguishes trade wars from trade disputes, where states use normal restrictive measures such as anti-dumping and countervailing within a framework of multilateral rules, and trade sanctions and embargoes, which are often more severe and driven by international political considerations. The restrictive measures used by states in a trade war are normally special, additional and punitive tariffs, which are intended to generate a negative impact on the original imports of goods and services from a certain trading partner. Indeed, a trade war often aims to exert influence over trade flows and therefore improve the balance of trade. However, there might be other objectives beyond trade, such as technology, industry and employment.

"Trade wars" are bilateral in nature, though more than two countries or economies could be involved in one conflict. Using tariffs and other economic means, states fight and retaliate against each other, and bargain and negotiate between themselves. These interactive characteristics demonstrate some similarities between a trade war and a real war. The imposition of tariffs and other unusual restrictive measures by a country are against the will of its trading partner, and these economic "weapons" are part of an arsenal for economic "warfare". As mentioned earlier, the tariffs are special, additional and punitive, and sometimes refer to the related legislation that provides legitimacy to their introduction.

The emphasis of economic means and objectives in the definition of trade wars does not mean that they are apolitical. On the contrary, trade wars are political both within a country and internationally. Within a country, domestic politics related to trade and trade protection can lead to policy decisions in favour of a trade war and affect policy stances for trade negotiations. Between countries, the initiation, escalation, de-escalation and finalization of trade wars involve a complicated process of international political interactions.

1.2 Trade wars and politics: a brief history

Early trade wars during the 17th–19th centuries

Historically speaking, trade wars often involved the world's major economic powers and trading nations, related to their rise and fall in the global landscape. Trade wars emerged as early as in the late medieval period, such as those between England and the Hanseatic League. During the 17th, 18th and 19th centuries, a number of major trade wars broke out, involving the world's major economies and trading nations at that time, such as the United Kingdom and France. These trade wars included, for instance, the Anglo-Dutch trade war and the Anglo-French trade war (see e.g. Conybeare, 1985, 1987). Rising nationalism, mercantilism and protectionism led to serious trade conflicts, as well as escalating warfare and shifting hegemony.

These early trade wars occurred within a broader economic and strategic context, sometimes involving the straightforward banning of imports and exports of certain goods. During 1615–1617, a brief trade war, due to the so-called Cockayne Project, was fought between England and the United Provinces of Holland (the Dutch Republic). The Anglo-Dutch trade war took place against the background of economic rivalry and military conflict between the two countries (Wilson, 1957). England banned the export of unfinished cloth, and the Dutch retaliated by banning the import of finished English cloth. The trade war later escalated to a broader commercial and geographical coverage, before the economic rivalry extended to naval warfare (Hinton,

1959). As a result, the Dutch economy was in a state of decline by the end of the 17th century, and so was its maritime and commercial supremacy.

There had long been economic conflicts between England and France. In 1664, Jean-Baptiste Colbert, the French minister of finance under Louis XIV, started to change the tariff system, which considerably raised tariffs on imported textiles. In 1666, English woolens were prohibited, and one year later, tariffs on textiles doubled. Colbert's policy efforts drew on the ideas of mercantilism, which sought to ensure that exports exceeded imports and thus to accumulate wealth. Colbertism has become a synonym of mercantilism and protectionism. England retaliated by raising duties on French wine and started to negotiate with the French side (Priestly, 1951). However, trade diplomacy did not work, and the Anglo-French trade war rapidly escalated. Despite efforts to end the trade war in the Treaty of Utrecht in 1713, bilateral tariffs remained high during most of the 18th century. After the 1820s, the trade relationship between the two countries started to improve. In 1836, particularly, the French side abolished some imports prohibitions and reduced tariffs on major British imports, such as cotton yarn, iron products and coal (Ratcliffe, 1978). Finally, the Cobden-Chevalier Treaty in 1860 led to, on the French side, the removal of all prohibitions and a general reduction of tariffs, and, on the British side, the admission of duty free goods except for French wine and spirits. In 1881, the treaty was replaced by a most-favoured nation (MFN) convention.

Evolving US trade policies since the beginning of the 20th century

The United States became the world's largest economy at the end of the 19th century, and then turned into the world's number one power after the two world wars. From the long-term historical perspective, the US trade policy has been constantly evolving, reflecting not only economic interest considerations and domestic politics, but also its global leadership and diplomatic influences.

During the first half of the 20th century, the US trade policy went through a fundamental transformation from protectionism to reciprocity, and then to the establishment of multilateral trading system. The 1922 Fordney-McCumber Tariff Act and the 1930 Hawley-Smoot Tariff Act raised the average tariffs by 20 and six percentage points, respectively. In particular, the introduction of the latter exacerbated the consequences of the Great Depression and put global trade into unprecedented difficulties. In the context of the New Deal, the 1934 Reciprocal Trade Agreements Act delegated powers over trade policy to the executive branch. By signing bilateral agreements, the US government started to guide tariffs towards a downward trend. Right before the end of World War II, the State Department began to plan a multilateral trade agreement. In 1947, 18 countries signed the General Agreement on Tariffs and Trade (GATT) in Geneva. A multilateral trade mechanism has been established based on the principles of non-discrimination and MFN treatment and is committed to lowering trade barriers.

The second half of the 20th century saw the evolution of US trade policy closely related to the advance of the global trading system. In the 1950s, efforts to promote free trade within the United States and at the multilateral level were not successful. In 1962, the Trade Expansion Act provided a legal basis for the United States to significantly reduce tariffs, leading to the success of the Kennedy Round – the sixth session of GATT multilateral trade negotiations held between 1964 and 1967. In the early 1970s, the world economy ushered in a turbulent era, as conflicts in international finance and trade intertwined, and the emerging trade deficit and rising unemployment reintroduced protectionism in the United States. In March 1973, the exchange rate system of the Bretton Woods system collapsed, and a floating exchange rate system debuted. At the end of the year, the oil crisis broke out. Afterwards, the Trade Act of 1974 to some extent completed the institutional construction of US trade policy, trying to accommodate both trade liberalization and protection in the same system. The Tokyo Round, which ended in 1979, further reduced tariff levels in developed countries. In the 1980s, with the rapid rise of trade deficit, the manufacturing industry was in dire straits, and with the rise of US trade protectionism, Japan became the primary target.

With the end of the Cold War in 1989, the US trade policy also entered a new era of promoting free trade and globalization. In 1991, the negotiations of the North American Free Trade Agreement (NAFTA) started, sparking unprecedented controversy in the United States. In November 1993, finally, the agreement was passed marginally by the Congress after heated debates. One month later, the seven-year-long Uruguay Round negotiations were successfully concluded, reshaping the rules system of the multilateral trading system. In January 1995, the Uruguay Round package entered into force and the World Trade Organization (WTO) was established. For China, the "GATT re-entry" negotiations that began in 1986 had turned into the "WTO accession" ones, while the bilateral negotiations with the United States became the key. In November 1999, the China–US Bilateral WTO Agreement was signed. In May 2000, the US Congress granted the "permanent normal trade relations" (PNTR) to China, which would not anymore be subject to annual MFN reviews according to the Jackson-Vanik Amendment to the Trade Act of 1974. In November 2001, China entered the WTO, which initiated the country's historic economic rise in the era of globalization. At the same time, the Doha Round of trade negotiations started, but unexpectedly fell into a deadlock.

In the context of the outbreak of the financial crisis in 2008 and the obstruction of multilateral trade negotiations, the US government focused its trade policy at the regional level and restarted negotiations on large-scale trade agreements. Negotiations on the Trans-Pacific Partnership (TPP) and the Transatlantic Trade and Investment Partnership kicked off in 2011 and 2013, respectively. Among the two mega agreements, TPP is related to the Obama administration's "Pivot to Asia" strategy and shows a "anyone but China" tendency. It finally completed negotiations in 2016.

After President Trump took office, under the "America First" principle, the US trade policy has undergone drastic changes – withdrawing from the TPP, revisiting the NAFTA (replacing it with the United States–Mexico–Canada Agreement, USMCA), and conducting bilateral trade negotiations with the European Union and Japan. The Trump administration advocates "fair and balanced trade" and emphasizes "mutually beneficial and reciprocal" economic relationships.[1] In particular, the administration shows concerns about the so-called "unfair trade advantages" of China and finally decided to fight a trade war against it. At the same time, the United States has shifted its focus to the bilateral level and adopted new principles of zero tariffs, zero non-tariff barriers and zero subsidies for its free trade negotiations. At the multilateral level, the United States also took serious actions – continuing to block the appointment of new judges of the Appellate Body, challenging "developing country status"[2] and setting the criteria for "market-oriented conditions" at the WTO.[3] In the meantime, a trilateral mechanism has been established since December 2017, involving the United States, the European Union and Japan. The Meeting of the Trade Ministers of the three major developed economies aims to enhance their cooperation in the WTO and in other forums, and to eliminate "unfair market distorting and protectionist practices by third countries".[4] The three parties have so far made clear their common goals and proposed actions with regard to, for instance, reforming WTO rules on industrial subsidies.

Throughout history, trade policy has been a highly politically sensitive issue in the United States. Relevant policies shift frequently between openness and protection, and the focus is constantly changing between bilateral, regional and multilateral levels. The protection of declining industries is a constant theme in US trade policy. Complex domestic political games are the main factors influencing trade legislation and policy making, which involve the relationship between bipartisan politics, Congress and the executive branch, as well as the influence of interest groups. Among many factors, the calculation on economic interests is decisive, but there are also foreign policy and ideological influences. The multilateral trading system was to some extent created by the United States after World War II, which has remained a dominant force since then. The system's evolution not only reflects the international game among WTO members, but is also affected by US domestic politics – the latter aspect should not be underestimated.

Trade wars fought by the United States

During the evolution of post-war US trade policy, the three dimensions of the multilateral trading system, regional trade agreements, and bilateral trade relations were intertwined. In terms of the third aspect, trade protection is a core issue, and involved industries have evolved: from textiles, to steel and home appliances, and then to automobiles and semiconductors. Empirical studies show that the scale of labour force and the level of import penetration of relevant industries are the main factors determining the degree of protection, while the two factors somehow reflect the degree of political influence on trade policy.

Among the protection measures, trade war is an extreme means. For the United States, whether to resort to a trade war depends on three factors: 1) the degree of tolerance of trade deficit, industrial damage and unemployment related increase in imports and the related force of political pressures; 2) the usefulness of "conventional" protective measures, such as trade remedies under the multilateral framework, and the effectiveness of bilateral negotiations; and 3) economic contextual factors, including business cycles and trends in exchange rate fluctuation. With regard to how to fight a trade war, the specific legal bases include, for instance, Section 232 of Trade Expansion Act of 1962, Section 301 of the Trade Act of 1974 and "Super 301" – an amendment by Section 1302 of the Omnibus Foreign Trade and Competitiveness Act of 1988.

Against the background of changes in domestic and international economic situations and political games, the United States has repeatedly provoked trade wars. It targeted either a specific trading partner or a group of them. In extreme cases, the unilateral, large-scale and general increase of tariffs can be considered as a trade war against all other countries, among which some of them will take retaliatory measures. This is true of the case of the Hawley-Smoot Tariff Act in 1930: the significant increase of US tariffs led to retaliation from Canada and some European countries and resulted in a widespread of protectionism. Since the 1970s, the United States launched trade wars mainly to restrict the import of specific products, which often involved specific trading nations. The negotiated compromises may include "voluntary export restraint", "orderly marketing arrangement" and commitments of market openness or currency appreciation. Several high-profile cases illustrate various possibilities for the evolution of trade wars (threats) and related negotiations:

- *After making threats, compromises were reached.* Typical examples are US trade conflicts with Japan over automobiles and semiconductors in the 1980s. In the early 1980s, Japan adopted automobile voluntary export restraint, facing the threat of import restrictions by the Reagan administration. In 1985, the United States launched a Section 301 investigation and an anti-dumping case against Japan for semiconductors. In order to avoid anti-dumping duties and retaliatory tariffs, Japan agreed in July 1986 to set a minimum price for its semiconductor exports and promised to increase the share of foreign companies in the country's semiconductor market. In January of the following year, the United States still imposed special tariffs on some Japanese products to urge Japan to comply.

- *After taking tariff measures, other parties made concessions.* This scenario is highlighted in the history of exchange rate disputes of the United States with other Western countries. In August 1971, the Nixon administration announced an additional tax of 10% on all imports as a temporary action to deal with "unfair exchange rates".[5] In December of that year, the United States reached the Smithsonian Agreement with Japan, Germany and other countries on the range of exchange rate adjustments, and the additional tax was therefore cancelled. In March 1973, the fixed exchange rate system established by the Bretton Woods system collapsed, and the world economy entered a new era of floating exchange rates. Due to the significant impact of exchange rates on international trade, the United States has frequently pressured other countries to appreciate their currencies, as realized in the Plaza Accord in September 1985.
- *Some measures led to countermeasures.* This was the case in the "Steel War" between the United States and Europe. In March 2002, the Bush administration imposed a temporary tariff of 8–30% on imported steel products, exempting Canada, Mexico and some developing countries. The European Union and other trading partners immediately resorted to the WTO dispute settlement mechanism and won the case in November 2003. With the United States insisting on maintaining tariffs, the European Union threatened to take retaliatory tariffs, and then the United States decided to withdraw the tariffs. A bilateral tariff war was avoided in this case. Back in the 1960s, however, the "chicken war" was a real tariff war – European Community members imposed tariffs on imports of chicken from the United States in 1962, and the Johnson administration imposed retaliatory tariffs on Europe in 1964.

The 1980s was the climax of the history of US trade protection, while Japan was the first target to be hit. Since the 1950s, Japanese companies had gained increasing shares in a wide range of American markets, starting from textiles to television, steel, motorcycles, automobiles and semiconductors (Schlossstein, 1984; Busch, 1999). Facing serious challenges in key industries such as automobiles and semiconductors in the 1980s, the US government complained bitterly about its Japanese counterpart's industrial policies and strategic trade policies (Section 1.3). Under great pressure from the United States, Japan had not only conducted arduous negotiations, but also made necessary compromises. Facing tariff threats, in particular, the Japanese government made considerable concessions in order to avoid the outbreak of large-scale trade wars. Its "voluntary export restraint" and other measures successfully eased the tension and in fact bought time for Japanese companies, whose increasing investment overseas, in Southeast Asia and especially in the United States, would finally ease trade conflicts.

However, Japan's lesson is equally worth learning, which is mainly reflected in the exchange rate issue closely related to trade. After President Reagan was re-elected in 1984, the new US Treasury Secretary Baker began to seek to devalue the US dollar through international agreements. On 22 September 1985, the United States reached an agreement with Japan, West Germany, Britain and France at the Plaza Hotel in New York on the appreciation of each country's currencies against the US dollar. Three months after the signing of the Plaza Accord, the Japanese yen rose rapidly by 20% against the US dollar and nearly doubled from 1:240 to 1:120 by the end of 1987. It is obvious that Japan's economy cannot afford such a sharp appreciation of its currency in the short term. More importantly, the long-term negative impact of yen appreciation on Japan's economy has been underestimated. Indeed, the sharp appreciation of the exchange rate and the continuous low level of interest rates contributed to an unprecedented bubble economy in the late 1980s and early 1990s, laying the seeds for the long-term economic downturn in Japan.

The trade war between the United States and China

Times have changed and history has pushed China into the "forefront" of trade conflicts. Against the background of intensified protectionist efforts and unilateral approaches, the United States started to fight a trade war against China in 2018. With regard to the context, the extent of China–US trade imbalance and the US pressure on China far exceeded the situation faced by Japan in the 1980s. In terms of the scope and scale, if the US–Japan trade conflict was basically maintained in a small part of the economy, or a limited number of sectors, the current China–US trade conflict has evolved into an all-round trade war.

In addition, it is far more than a trade war. The US–Japan trade conflict in the 1980s took place in the conventional trade background. Its basic pattern was that Japanese enterprises produced locally and then exported their products to the United States. The current China–US trade war takes place against the background of globalization (Chapter 2, Section 2.1), which has been characterized by a strong wave of FDI flows and production off-shoring after the end of the Cold War. Between 1990 and 2018, worldwide FDI stock had surged from US$ 1.7 trillion to US$ 32.3 trillion.[6] China has been a major beneficiary of FDI flows and the associated production relocation. A large number of multinational enterprises (MNEs) from the United States, Europe, Japan, South Korea, Taiwan Province of China and other advanced economies use China as their production base and export platform, and they account for a considerable portion of China's exports and surplus with the United States. Since the mid-2000s, the proportion of foreign-invested enterprises (FIEs) in China's exports has dropped consider-ably, but it remains at a relatively high level. The latest data show that about 40% of China's exports and about 60% of its exports to the United States come from FIEs.

Why does this unprecedented trade war break out and what are its impli-cations? Some studies on the China–US trade tensions in general have been undertaken, covering the following aspects. First, regarding the causes of the trade tensions, trade imbalance (Lin and Wang, 2018), domestic policy pres-sure (Bhidé and Phelps, 2005) and technological catch-up (Yang et al., 2018) have been investigated. Second, a number of studies explore the effects of the trade frictions (Dong and Whalley, 2012; Gompert et al., 2016; Rosyadi and Widodo, 2017; Guo et al., 2018). Third, some discuss how to mitigate trade frictions, including by using WTO rules and dispute settlement mecha-nisms (Ren, 2017), deepening reforms to further improve China's economic system (Yu and Li, 2004), adopting free trade agreements (Feng et al., 2018), participating in the reconfiguration of global value chains (Huang, 2018) and improving the quality of export products (Zhang et al., 2018).

Some scholars have conducted specific studies on the China–US trade war started in 2018. At the macro level, Li et al. (2018) quantified and simu-lated the possible effect of the China–US trade war on both countries and other economies by constructing a general multi-country equilibrium model. Amiti et al. (2019a) explored how the change of trade policies in the United States influence prices and welfare. Lu et al. (2019) investigated the effect of the China–US trade war on the welfare of the two sides based on their lists of taxed products. At the micro level, for instance, Huang et al. (2018) assessed the market response of companies in the two countries to the trade war between the United States and China. However, comprehensive studies on the China–US trade war are still missing.

1.3 Theories of trade wars

The theoretical research on trade wars involves three major main ques-tions: 1) why trade wars occur; 2) what the interactive process is and how it determines the outcome of the trade war; and 3) what the impacts of the trade war are. From a practical point of view, the three questions are intertwined and interrelated. Why a trade war occurred is an international economic issue but is also related to international relations and politics. The former reflects the economic causes of a trade war, while the latter examines political interactions between countries and among various interest groups within a country. Looking into the literature of international trade, theories on optimal tariff, strategic trade policy and cooperative and noncooperative trade policy making have shed light on the interactive nature of trade policy making, including through the extreme form of trade wars. Regarding the impact of trade war, conventional trade theory explains well its price and welfare effects. The question of how the trade war is fought, why tit-for-tat retaliations happen and what determines the result can be studied with the help of useful analytical tools of game theory.

Trade theory: difference perspectives

The research in the field of international trade has been concerned about trade frictions for a long period. Traditional free trade theory holds that free trade can maximize global welfare, and a country's unilateral trade liberalization can maximize its own welfare. Therefore, trade frictions worsen a country's welfare, and no country can profit in a tariff war (Gros, 1987). However, some scholars argue that under certain conditions welfare with tariffs imposed is better than that under free trade.

In the late 19th century, Edgeworth (1894) first introduced the idea that an optimal level of tariff maximizes a country's welfare. In the mid-20th century, Johnson (1954) and Gorman (1957) analyzed the optimal tariff issue under the framework of pure exchange of two goods between two countries. Johnson finds that a country tends to gain in a tariff war if its import price elasticity is significantly higher than that in the other country. When the scope for this gain is wide, its export goods approximate a pure luxury in world consumption. Gorman (1957) extends Johnson's study and illustrates that if the other country does not retaliate, welfare under tariffs is better than under free trade. Tower (1975) and Bhagwati and Srinivasan (1976) loosen the assumption of no retaliation. Whalley (1958) reveals that the tariff war between countries with the same size would damage both sides, whereas tariff wars between countries of different sizes would benefit the large one but damage the small one. Markusen and Wigle (1989) find that the United States has virtually similar welfare under Nash Equilibrium tariff and free trade, whereas Canada has better welfare under free trade than under tariff.

In the 1980s, the development of new trade theory based on imperfectly competitive markets and economies of scale led to the emergence of new theoretical approaches. Brander and Spencer (1985) introduce the concept of "strategic trade policy" indicating that a country's government can adopt certain trade protection measures, such as trade subsidies and tariffs, which can help protect domestic industries from strong international shock. Strategic trade policy can improve the competitive position of domestic enterprises in the international market. In addition, the policy promotes the transfer of profits from incompletely competitive industries, particularly oligopolistic competitive industries, and thereby improving the overall national welfare brought by trade benefits. Brander and Spencer (1985) argue that if a country does not retaliate against the export subsidy of a foreign country, the subsidy will provide a competitive advantage to foreign firms. Consequently, foreign firms increase their output, whereas domestic firms reduce their output. The profits of foreign firms increase by more than the amount of the export subsidy, and the foreign country gains welfare.

Krugman (1986) further developed a systematic international trade theory. This theory constructs a model involving three countries, which have similar goals that maximize their own economic benefits. Two of the product-exporting countries have formed an oligopoly structure in the supply market and follow the Cournot game framework. To maximize the economic benefits in the Cournot game of the oligopoly market structure, both countries will actively adopt export subsidy policies that form an equilibrium similar to the Prisoner's Dilemma. Thus, the policy choice for maximizing the economic benefits of both sides aims to abandon the export product subsidy policy at the same time, but the final stable equilibrium results in the adoption of a subsidy policy. The overall welfare of international trade has been maximized. Therefore, product-exporting countries should minimize the level of export subsidies through negotiations, whereas product-importing countries do the opposite. Dixit (1988) demonstrates that the best domestic response to foreign export subsidies is typically a partial offset of tariffs. Collie (1991, 1994) extends the analysis of retaliation with a countervailing tariff and finds that no profit shifting argument for an export subsidy exists when the foreign country faces retaliation.

Several scholars have formulated theories showing that trade frictions can also arise from endogenous political processes. Early studies assumed that the government would maximize national welfare without the consideration of private interests. Johnson (1954) examines the process of how the policy interdependence between governments is modelled as the non-cooperative equilibrium of a tariff game between two countries. Mayer (1981) and Riezman (1982) discuss negotiated trade agreements in a similar approach to Johnson (1954) and regard it as the equilibrium result of a bargaining game model between the two governments. Kuga (1973) provides a general statement of existence regarding tariff distorted equilibria, which has been missing from previous literature, and uses a multi-country, multi-good framework that proves the existence of a Nash Equilibrium supported by retaliatory tariffs.

The analysis of international trade can find useful tools from interest group behaviours in several cases at the national level (Kindleberger, 1951). Peltzman (1976) indicates that the government rarely pursues policies that maximize economic welfare but seeks those policies that maximize political support, thereby generally reflecting the interests of those influential interest groups. Grossman and Helpman (1995) develop a model to shed light on the determinants of the structure of protection in noncooperative and cooperative policy equilibrium with the consideration of influences of special interest groups on national policies, which can also help predict the outcome of trade negotiations between two countries.

There have been several quantitative analyses on cooperative and noncooperative trade policies. Perroni and Whalley (2000) provide estimates of noncooperative tariffs in a simple Armington model that features traditional terms-of-trade effects. Ossa (2011) provides such estimates in a simple Krugman model that features trade production relocation effects. Broda et al. (2008) provide detailed estimates of the inverse export supply elasticities faced by a number of non-WTO member countries. Ossa (2014) quantitatively analyzes cooperative and noncooperative trade policies using the data covering seven regions and 33 industries based on the general equilibrium model that combines intra-industry trade, inter-industry trade, and political influence. He finds that optimal tariffs average 62%, world trade war tariffs average 63%, and the government welfare losses from a breakdown of international trade policy cooperation average 3%.

Trade theory: price and welfare effects of a trade war

The conventional trade theory is a useful framework to understand the basic economic effects of the trade war. We present a simple model to describe the price and welfare effects under the situation of imposing tariffs. Assume that there are only two countries: Country A (home country) and Country B (foreign country), which are both large countries that can influence world prices. Besides, only two products are available in the market: cotton (C) and fleece (F). These two products are perfectly substituted for each other, which means they are identical to consumers and income would be spent either on cotton or fleece. We further assume that Country A imports fleece and exports cotton, while Country B imports cotton and exports fleece.

To examine the price effect, we introduce the concept of "terms of trade", which refers to the ratio of a country's export price to its import price. For Country A, the terms of trade should be defined as the ratio of cotton price to fleece price, while for Country B they are vice versa. Under the model assumptions of two countries and two goods, we can depict an initial equilibrium, where relative supply (RS^1) of cotton to fleece and relative demand (RD^1) of these two goods are equal (point E1 in Figure 1.1), and the relative price of cotton at equilibrium is $(P_C/P_F)^1$. When Country A imposes a tariff on imported fleece, the relative price of fleece to the price of cotton increases for domestic consumers. To benefit from the higher price, domestic producers will produce fleece instead of cotton, so the relative supply of cotton decreases from RS^1 to RS^2. As domestic consumers will pay a relative lower price for cotton and are thus more willing to switch to cotton consumption, the relative demand of cotton rises from RD^1 to RD^2. Then, we have a new equilibrium E2 at the intersection of RS^2 and RD^2. Comparing the new equilibrium price $(P_C/P_F)^2$ with the initial one $(P_C/P_F)^1$, we can conclude that the relative price of cotton to fleece increases, namely, the terms of trade in Country A improve.

Then we explain the reasons why countries impose tariffs from the perspective of welfare. We first introduce two terms: consumer surplus and producer surplus. They are economic measures of consumer benefits and producer benefits, respectively. On a supply demand curve, the former is the area between the equilibrium price and the demand curve, and the latter is the area between the equilibrium price and the supply curve. We only consider one product – fleece – which is imported by Country A and exported

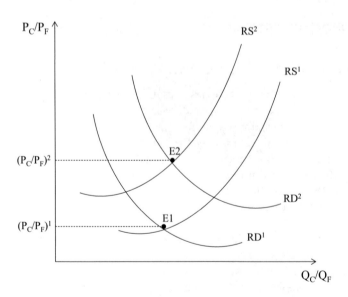

Figure 1.1 Trade wars: the price effect of special tariffs

by Country B. Given the initial point of world equilibrium price P_W, we depict fleece supply S^1 and demand D^1 in Country A (Figure 1.2). When Country A imposes tariff τ on fleece, the import price increases from P_W to P_T, and the export price of Country B decreases from P_W to P^*_T, where $P_W = (1 + \tau)P^*_T$. At the new price P_T, the supply rises from S^1 to S^2 and demand falls from D^1 to D^2. Thus, the area of $a + b + c + d$ represents the loss of consumer surplus in Country A, and a represents the producer surplus. Government revenues can be expressed by $c + e$, specifically, c is revenues from import tariff and e is the terms of trade gains. Therefore, the net effect of import tariff is $c + e + a - (a + b + c + d) = e - b - d$. When tariff τ is small, the area e will be considerably larger than $b + d$, and Country A will consequently benefit from the tariff policy, and vice versa.

The game theoretical approach

Unilateral trade restrictions lead to income gains, but when retaliations take place, income losses appear. Emphasizing the interactive nature of trade wars, game theory helps describe their process and predict the outcome. It investigates the decision making of the two involved countries, explains the rationale behind their strategic choices and identifies potential dominant strategies in a variable-sum game – which is normally the case in a

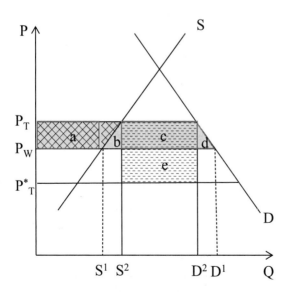

Figure 1.2 Trade wars: the welfare effect of special tariffs

trade war. For the two parties, fighting a trade war can be a static game or a dynamic one that incorporates the effects of time. A static game involves players who make decisions simultaneously. In the reality of a trade war, however, the game of imposing tariffs is often played in a sequential manner. In addition, we need to think of the iteration of games, or a game that is being played over a number of time periods, which makes it dynamic.

Static game

Similarly, we assume that two countries are engaged in a trade war: Country A and Country B. Both play the game of trade war with two choices: Tariff (T) and No tariff (N), or in normal game theoretical terms, Defection or Cooperate. Their different choices yield four different outcomes: $T_A T_B$, $T_A N_B$, $N_A N_B$ and $N_A T_B$. For the two countries, the payoffs of these four outcomes are presented in the following payoff matrix. The question is how the value of payoffs (utility) is decided in the context of a trade war. From a purely trade perspective, the value can be considered as the real export loss, which depends mainly on the volume of exports affected by the special tariffs and the degree of the tariffs imposed. In reality, the picture is more complicated, as many other factors than real export loss are considered. In addition, there are not only the problem of actual influences, but also the problem of cognition and subjective judgement of influences. In other words, the decision makers' prediction of and attached importance to specific economic variables, such as export amount, economic growth rate, employment and stock market performance, affect their perceived value of utility.

		Country B	
		Not to impose tariffs	To impose tariffs
Country A	Not to impose tariffs	$\left(N_A^N, N_B^N\right)$	$\left(N_A^T, T_B^N\right)$
	To impose tariffs	$\left(T_A^N, N_B^T\right)$	$\left(T_A^T, T_B^T\right)$

Assume only exports count for the two countries, and then the value of payoffs is reflected in real export loss, which is determined by the amount of affected exports, the rate of tariffs and two other factors. One is the degree of tariff pass-through, or how the exports price changes in reaction to the special tariffs. We introduce the term of "tariff pass-through rate" to describe the sensitivity of changes in export commodity prices with respect to changes in tariffs. The rate is normally less than 1, as the exporters would lower the pre-tax prices of export commodities in order to maintain their market. The other factor is the price elasticity of demand, a measure of how much the export volume will change in response to the change in export commodity prices caused by extra tariffs.

Suppose that the volume of Country A's affected exports to Country B is π_A and Country B's affected exports to Country A is π_B; the tariff pass-through rates of Country A and Country B are θ_A and θ_B; and the price elasticity of demand for exports of Country A and Country B is a and b, respectively. In addition, assume that the benefits from imposing tariffs for Country A and Country B are respectively β and ε of the amount of their initial imports.

For Country B, consider the outcome of $T_A N_B$ – Country A chooses to impose tariffs, while Country B chooses not to do so. Suppose that Country A imposes tariffs on Country B's exports at the level of S_A, then the price of Country B's exports would increase by $S_A \theta_B$ because of tariff pass-through. Further considering the price elasticity of demand for exports, we can calculate the change of exports of Country B is b $\times S_A \theta_B$, which means that the exports will decrease by about $bS_A \theta_B$. Therefore, the change of export volume of Country B is: $\pi_B[(1 + S_A \theta_B) \times (1 - bS_A \theta_B) - 1] = \pi_B S_A \theta_B (1 - b - bS_A \theta_B)$. Accordingly, in the situation $T_A N_B$, of Country B's payoff $\upsilon_B(T_A N_B) = \pi_B S_A \theta_B (1 - b - bS_A \theta_B)$. For Country A, it could benefit from imposing tariff on Country B. Thus, Country A's payoff of $\upsilon_A(T_A N_B) = \beta \pi_B$. In the payoff matrix shown earlier, the payoffs of Country A and Country B are also expressed as $(T_A^N N_B^T)$. Similarly, other outcomes can also be calculated and expressed.

Based on different choices of the two countries, we can generate four outcomes and the associated configurations of payoffs. We can then depict them in a two-dimensional utility space (U_A, U_B). Apart from several rather rare scenarios,[7] there are three common game structures: Prisoner's Dilemma, Chicken and Stag Hunt (Figure 1.3).

- *Prisoner's Dilemma.* The most common game structure is Prisoner's Dilemma, where Country A has the preference ordering $T_A N_B > N_A N_B > T_A T_B > N_A T_B$, whereas Country B has $N_A T_B > N_A N_B > T_A T_B > T_A N_B$. The dominant strategy for either country is T, which indicates that both countries would impose tariffs regardless of their speculation about the action of their counterparts. When two large countries engage in trade wars, they commonly impose tariffs on each other, which results in losses for both. The trade theory posits that if Country A imposes tariffs on Country B but Country B fails to take retaliatory action, then the terms of trade in Country A would improve. Thus, the payoff of Country A with imposing tariffs unilaterally would increase compared with without imposing tariffs. For Country B, the export volume to Country A would decline, and the export price would also decrease for maintaining their market. Therefore, the payoff of Country B when the tariff is unilaterally imposed would be

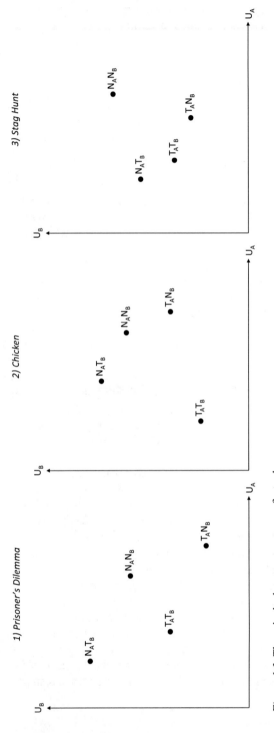

Figure 1.3 The principal game structures of a trade war

lower than that of Country B without tariffs. This scenario is similar to the context of Country B that unilaterally imposes tariffs on Country A. If both countries impose tariffs, then either country would suffer from damages due to tariffs imposed by the other, while benefiting from the tariffs imposed on the other. Thus, the payoffs of both sides with imposing tariffs are lower than those in the case of imposing tariffs unilaterally.

- *Chicken*. This game structure implies that mutual defection is the worst choice for the two countries. In this case, imposing tariffs on each other generates the worst results for both sides in a trade war. Country A has the preference ordering $T_AN_B > N_AN_B > N_AT_B > T_AT_B$. In this game, if Country A believes that Country B would not impose tariffs, it should impose tariffs; if Country A believes that Country B would impose tariffs, it should not impose tariffs. This does not occurs often in the trade area. The most possible situation is a trade war between two relatively small countries, which merely harms their domestic revenues by imposing retaliatory tariffs.
- *Stag Hunt*. The game structure implies that coordinated cooperation exists if all parties involved are desperate for collaboration.[8] In a trade war, Country A has the preference ordering $N_AN_B > T_AN_B > T_AT_B > N_AT_B$, whereas Country B has the preference ordering $N_AN_B > N_AT_B > T_AT_B > T_AN_B$. Thus, both countries would collaborate as long as both think that their counterpart has understood the positive effect of cooperation. Different from the previously mentioned game structures, Stag Hunt typically requires that both parties observe the return of other strategies. Both parties would be encouraged to further cooperate when they observe the benefits of non-cooperation. Therefore, the Stag Hunt could possibly become the result of the several stages of retaliatory tariffs.

Dynamic game

A game can be dynamic for two reasons. First, the interaction between players may be inherently sequential. Thus, players can observe the actions of other players before deciding upon their optimal response. Second, a game is dynamic if a one-off game is repeated a number of times, and players observe the outcome of previous games prior to playing subsequent games. In the real-world scenario of a trade war, players' actions are sequential, and the late player can observe other players' actions prior to making its own decisions. In addition, all players can possibly communicate with each other, observe each other's behaviours, alter their actions and consequently reach an agreement.

With consideration of the dynamic game, economists are highly interested in repeated games, where players are assumed to have numerous opportunities to observe their counterparts and coordinate their actions. Both finite repeated games and infinite repeated games exist. A repeated game that will end after a certain number of iterations is called a finite repeated game. Games that may be repeated forever are infinite repeated games. In the case of trade wars, the former refers to a trade warfare with many rounds of "combats", or tariff actions, and a final ending of tariff withdrawal. The latter is similar to a situation when tariffs are imposed, adjusted and last for a long time. Cooperation may be possible in infinitely repeated games but may be impossible under certain situations with finitely repeated games.

A substantial number of theoretical and empirical studies have proven that sequentially played Prisoner's Dilemma may develop cooperative patterns of interaction. The effect of time is a critical issue. Olson and Bailey (1981) argued that decision makers commonly attach less emphasis to future payoffs than to current payoffs. That is, their time preference rate is positive. As long as the players in the repeated Prisoner's Dilemma do not over-underestimate the future payoff, believing the cumulative discounted value of the future cooperation may surpass the value of current betrayal, they may adopt cooperative strategies. Similarly, cooperating in sequential Chicken and Stag Hunt game structures, particularly the latter one, is possible. Overall, repeated and sequential games can provide players with the necessary information to help them realize the benefits of cooperation and coordinate them for collaborations, and countries need to consider the future evolution of the game of a trade war (and the discounted value of future payoffs) for the right decision at the current time.

Notes

1 "Securing Fair and Balanced Trade for the American People", *The While House*, 28 September 2008.
2 "An Undifferentiated WTO: Self-Declared Development Status Risks Institutional Irrelevance", *Communication from the United States*, 15 January 2019; Memorandum on Reforming Developing-Country Status in the World Trade Organization, Presidential Memorandum issued on 26 July 2019.
3 "The Importance of Market-Oriented Conditions to the World Trading System", *Draft General Council Decision, Communication from the United States*, 20 February 2020.
4 Joint Statement by the United States, European Union and Japan at MC11, Buenos Aires, 12 December 2017.
5 Speech by President Nixon on 15 August 1971.
6 Data source: UNCTAD.
7 Others game structures, such as Hawk-Dove (Smith, 1982), Deadlock, and Bully (Snyder and Diesing, 1977), are not common in the case of trade wars.
8 The game structure is derived from a story in the book *Discours sur l'origine et les fondements de l'inégalité parmi les hommes* by Jean-Jacques Rousseau.

2 The China–US trade war

Context and cause

War is the continuation of politics by other means.

– Carl von Clausewitz

China and the United States have been engaged in a trade war since mid-2018. A vertical comparison shows that the current China–US trade war is unprecedented. On the one hand, the scale of exports and imports affected, and the range of commodities involved are enormous. After the outbreak and escalation of the China–US trade war, the record level of affected trade flows has been elevated from billions of dollars in the past to hundreds of billions of dollars now. Earlier trade wars often targeted one or more specific types of products, while the China–US trade war has involved a massive number of commodities without distinction. On the other hand, the trade war takes place in an era of globalization, which means that its impacts are far beyond trade. Why did such a trade war come about between the world's two largest economies together accounting for more than 40% of the global economy? How has the bilateral conflict been involved to such an extent that it hit the world economy hard? What have been the context and cause of such a conflict? These are major questions that this chapter tries to shed light on.

2.1 The global context: from globalization to de-globalization?

The scale of the China–US trade war is unprecedented, and it is the first major trade war in the era of globalization – a strong wave of "economic globalization" started in the early 1990s after the end of the Cold War. In a broader sense, the concept of "economic globalization" refers to the process of deepening economic ties and increasing interdependence among countries. At the national level, it is manifested as an increase in economic openness and internationalization; worldwide, it is exhibited as countries conducting international economic exchanges in increasingly in-depth ways, and it is also reflected in intensified cross-border flows of goods, services, capital, personnel and information. In this sense, the history of globalization can be traced back to the Age of Discovery, if not earlier. In the second half of the 20th century, globalization can be divided into two stages: during the Cold War era, a "partial globalization" within the Western world and with the active involvement of a rather limited number of developing economies; after the end of the Cold War, a "strong globalization" at the global level, with the proactive participation of major developing countries and emerging economies (Liang, 2017).

The driving forces of globalization include many aspects. Technical advancement reduces transaction costs by deciding the costs of transportation, information transmission, production and operation, thereby "pushing" the international operation of enterprises. Of particular importance are those "general purpose technologies" that have a wide range of influences. Institutional factors determine the level of tariffs and non-tariff barriers in the area of trade, and the level of market access and investor protection in terms of investment, thereby "pulling" the international operations of enterprises in these two aspects. The GATT/WTO principles of non-discrimination and reciprocity as formalized by Bagwell and Staiger (1999) have played an important role in enhancing efficiency at the global level. Globalization can be measured in two major areas: real economy – as reflected by international trade in goods and services – and finance – as reflected in cross-border flows of capital.

The wave of strong globalization started to rise rapidly in the 1990s and reached its climax in the first decade of the 21st century. This is reflected in both the real economy and finance at the global level (Figure 2.1):

- *Real economy*. From the early 1990s, international trade (including trade in both goods and services) began to show significant growth that continued until 2008. Accordingly, the total amount of international trade increased from US$ 4 trillion in 1989 to US$ 8 trillion in 2000 and then to US$ 20 trillion in 2008. From a relative level, the ratio of total international trade to total world economic output (the sum of GDP of all countries) increased from 18% in 1989 to 32% in 2008.
- *Finance*. International capital flows, including FDI, international portfolio and other investment (mainly bank lending), also began to grow rapidly since the 1990s. Accordingly, the total amount of international capital flows soared from about US$ 1 trillion in the mid-1990s to nearly US$ 10 trillion in 2007. Its ratio to the total output of the world economy (the total GDP of all countries) has increased from about 5% to 22%.

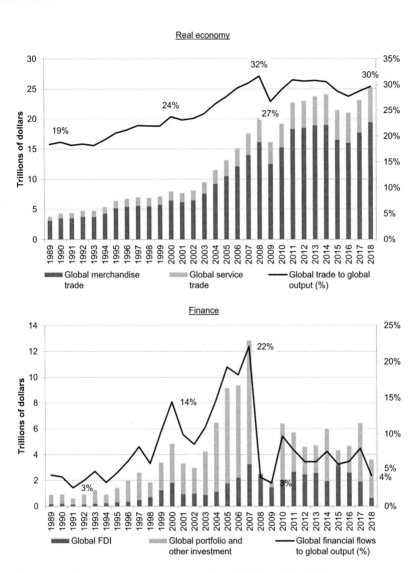

Figure 2.1 Globalization after the end of the Cold War, 1989–2018
Source: Adapted and updated from Liang (2017).

The impact of this wave of globalization is unprecedented, making it possible to redraw the global economic landscape. As the world's largest economy, largest importer and largest exporter of capital, the United States played the most important role in promoting globalization. In addition,

China, India and other major emerging economies and developing countries have embraced globalization, bringing billions of people into the global system of division of labour, and thus contributing to the large-scale transfer of productive capacity from developed to developing countries. However, the distribution of the benefits of globalization is not balanced, as there are winners and losers in the increasingly intensified global competition. Accompanying globalization is the polarization between the rich and the poor, which may occur both among countries and among different parts of societies within a country.

Since the early 1990s, the degree of internationalization of both real economy and finance has increased rapidly, but the strength and speed of the latter is much higher than that of the former. International capital flows have been highly volatile, and their ups and downs are in sharp contrast to the relatively stable increase in the internationalization of the real economy. This has become an important source of world economic risks, apart from the enhanced global imbalances in terms of the production/consumption and export/import patterns.

In 2008, the global financial crisis broke out, leading to a major setback for the world economy and its globalization process (Figure 2.1). Technological and institutional factors had jointly pushed forward the process of strong globalization before, but the thrust from the latter has obviously weakened after the crisis. Correspondingly, the momentum of globalization has changed from strong to weak: this is first manifested in the sharp decline in global financial capital flows, but also in the slow recovery and later weak growth of international trade and FDI flows.

The rising populism in some Western countries became an unexpected political aftermath of the economic crisis. This can be considered as a political response to the economics problems related to the crisis. Globalization has become an "ideal" target of criticism, while major winners during the unprecedented wave of strong globalization between 1989 and 2008 have become the "natural" scapegoats. In some countries, this is manifested in a rising nationalism and a growing anti-globalization sentiment, which have significantly affected economic policy making. In countries like the United States, there has been a paradigm shift in domestic politics and international economic policies. "America First" means a stronger focus on the economic interest of the United States, and in the meantime less responsibilities for the global system. For the rest of the world, such a paradigm shift may imply rising unilateralism and protectionism.

In recent years, globalization has further weakened, and a symptom of "de-globalization" in both real economy and finance has emerged (Figure 2.1). Major events that highlighted this trend were Brexit and policy changes in the United States. There have been some reverse changes of the institutional factors that had originally promoted globalization. The rise of tariffs related to the trade disputes and trade wars is an apparent example. These changes have resulted in distortions of market mechanisms and potential reversals of firms' decisions on international sourcing and production offshoring. In addition, the deadlock in the multilateral trading system has made things worse. At the global level, de-globalization is reflected in the "reverse" flows of resources, especially the return of industrial production capacity – the so-called "reshoring" – and flow of international capital from developing to developed countries.

2.2   China–US trade relationship: interdependencies and imbalances

The strong wave of globalization after the end of the Cold War coincided with China's renewed efforts in market reform and economic opening up. Especially after its accession to the WTO, huge international markets and external resources have promoted the rapid growth of China's exports. These resources have been highlighted by rapidly rising FDI inflows, which brings in an invaluable package of foreign capital, advanced technology, management knowhow and foreign market access opportunities, enhances domestic competition and promotes industrial development (Liang, 2004). In the meantime, China has rapidly penetrated the American market, and the two countries have developed a trade relationship characterized by both strong interdependencies and huge imbalances. Trade relations are the core of complex economic relations between China and the United States. The evolution of China–US trade relations has reshaped China, the United States and even the world economy.

Unbalanced trade relationship between China and the United States

China's rise on the global trade arena during the reform era has been phenomenal. In 1990, China's export volume was US$ 62 billion – 1.8% of the global total. In 2000, it quadrupled to US$ 250 billion – 3.9% of the global total. After joining the WTO, China's exports grew at an extremely high speed, soaring to US$ 1.43 trillion in 2008, accounting for 8.9% of the world's total exports. After the onset of the global financial crisis, China's total export volume and its share in the global market continued to increase. A decade later, its total exports reached US$ 2.48 trillion, or 12.7% of the world's total. Such a high "market share" in global trade was only achieved by the United States in the late 1960s. The enhancement of the international competitiveness of Chinese economy and the stable and open international markets have jointly contributed to the rise of China's exports. From the latter aspect, the United States is one of the decisive factors.

The growth of China–US trade is asymmetrical. In terms of the overall size of trade, the import and export volume of the United States was four times that of China in 2000, and the two countries were even in 2012. In terms of total exports, those from the United States only doubled from 2000 to 2013, while those from China increased eight times. Chinese statistics show that before the global financial crisis, the proportion of the United States in China's total exports remained at the level of 20%~21%. After that, the specific gravity dropped to 17%~18% (Figure 2.2). US statistics show that China's share of total US imports doubled from 2000 to 2007 to 16%, then increased to 22% in 2017 – the year before the outbreak of the trade war.

There has always been a serious imbalance in China–US trade. Statistics from China show that the United States has contributed US$ 3.1 trillion, nearly three-quarters of China's accumulated trade surplus of US$ 4.2 trillion since its WTO accession. The monetary effects of the imbalanced trade relationship between the United States and China is apparent. China has accumulated a huge amount of so-called "China dollars", a considerable part of which has been invested in the US treasury bond market (Liang, 2017). This follows the same path of petrodollars; money earned from trade is "recycled" back to the United States. What is different in China is that, because of the foreign exchange regime, the Chinese Central Bank bought in all foreign currencies that entered the country through trade and FDI, which became a dominant channel of money supply within the Chinese economy. The situation has been changed only since the mid-2010s due to large capital outflows.

The role of the United States in contributing to China's trade surplus has changed, but it is basically in a dominant position. This can be seen from the four stages from 2001 to 2018: 1) during 2001–2005, the annual trade surplus between China and the United States increased rapidly from less than US$ 30 billion to more than US$ 110 billion, and the total China–US trade surplus was US$ 324 billion, which was 1.5 times the total Chinese surplus during the period; 2) from 2006 to 2010, China–US trade surplus totalled US$ 803 billion, accounting for 72% of China's total surplus; 3) from 2011 to 2015, China–US trade surplus reached US$ 1135 billion, or 70% of China's total surplus, while the proportion of the United States continued to decline, from 131% in 2011 to 44% in 2015; 4) from 2016 to 2018, China–US trade surplus amounted to about US$ 850 billion, nearly two-thirds of China's total surplus, and the US share rose rapidly, from 49% in 2016 to 95% in 2018.

From the perspective of the United States, China is a major source of trade deficit, the importance of which has been constantly increasing.

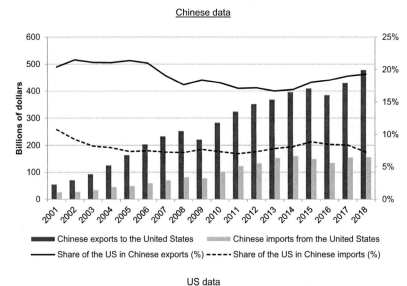

Chinese data

Chinese exports to the United States ████ Chinese imports from the United States
—— Share of the US in Chinese exports (%) ----- Share of the US in Chinese imports (%)

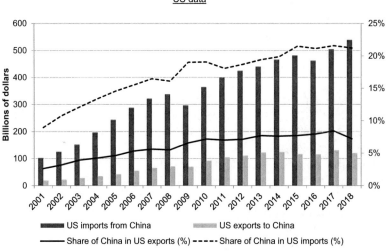

US data

US imports from China ████ US exports to China
—— Share of China in US exports (%) ----- Share of China in US imports (%)

Figure 2.2 China–US trade after China's WTO accession, 2001–2018
Source: Adapted and updated from Liang (2017).

Trade deficit between the United States and China had increased from US$ 83 billion in 2001 to US$ 366 billion in 2015, accounting for half of the total trade deficit of the United States. In 2018, although a trade war broke out in the second half of the year, the US trade deficit with China rose to an all-time high of about US$ 420 billion. It is worth noting that there are differences in trade statistics between China and the United States, especially regarding the amount of China's exports to the United States. The number shown by the Chinese statistics is smaller than that of the United States.

With regard to China–US bilateral trade in goods, China has enjoyed a long-lasting large surplus. However, the US economy has benefited greatly from its trade with China. A very wide range of high-quality and low-price Chinese products have been imported, bringing significant welfare benefits to ordinary American consumers, especially after China's accession to the WTO (Amiti et al., 2017). To some extent, they also became an important force in keeping inflation down. In terms of American exports, China has become one of the fastest growing markets for US exports. Its share of US exports has increased from 2% in 2000 to 8% in recent years. Since 2007, China has become the third largest export market of the United States, after Canada and Mexico, and the growth potential is very high.

Understanding the trade interdependencies and imbalances

A Section 301 investigation launched in August 2017 against China was the "prelude" of the China–US trade war (Chapter 3). This investigation targeted technological issues, which can be considered as the direct cause of the trade war. However, a basic logic of the investigation is that China's acts, policies and practices on science and technology may inhibit US exports, thus widening its trade deficit. More importantly, the investigation took place against the background of a very large and persistent trade imbalance between China and the United States, which has become a major excuse for the latter to fight a trade war. In addition, increasing exports and reducing trade deficit have become an important demand of the US side in its trade diplomacy with China. Thus, an objective understanding of trade imbalance is a key issue in analyzing the context and cause of the China–US trade war.

Indeed, the imbalance in China–US trade in goods is very large in scale. However, the real problem of imbalance in China–US trade in goods is not as serious as the United States claims because of the following reasons:

- *Statistical differences.* Due to the difference in the statistical systems, China's figures of the surplus with the United States is significantly smaller than the United States' number of deficits with China. In the early 2000s, the difference was about US$ 50 billion, while in recent years the difference was about US$ 100 billion. The differences were due to two reasons: first, Chinese exports are re-exported to the United States through a third place, and Chinese statistics show that they are exported to the third place, while American statistics attribute them to

China according to the principle of origin; second, the prices of China's export declaration and the United States' import declaration can be different, especially in the mode of contract manufacturing and processing trade.

- *Global value chain perspective.* China's exported goods often contain many imported parts and components, while trade statistics take account of the total price of these products. In the area of processing trade, in particular, some products only complete the assembly process in China. Therefore, the size of local value addition is often very small. Overall domestic added value accounts for a bit above 60% of China's total exports, far below the levels of more than 70% in the case of United States and more than 80% in the cases of Japan and Germany.
- *Exports by Chinese affiliates of foreign companies.* China is a major production and export platform for foreign companies from many countries and regions, thus bearing the "blame" for their trade surplus with the United States. The prevalence of contract manufacturing means that some American companies also produce in China and export the products to the United States. Statistically speaking, although the proportion of FIEs in China's total exports has significantly declined, it is still as high as 40% in recent years. In the ranking of China's largest exporters, some FIEs have always maintained a leading position.

While China enjoys a very large surplus in trade in goods with the United States, its deficit in trade in services with the United States is sizeable and increasing. US service exports to China have increased fivefold since the mid-2000s, with a trade surplus of US$ 56 billion in 2016. China's total deficit in trade in service amounted to above US$ 240 billion that year, the largest in the world. In the following two years, China's trade deficit in services with the United States narrowed to US$ 54 billion and 49 billion, respectively. Overall, the potential of growth of services exports from the United States to China is promising, and the US surplus with China in this area will grow in the years to come.

Another often neglected deficit on the Chinese side is related to the size of revenues from foreign affiliates. According to data of the US Department of Commerce, sales of majority-owned US affiliates of Chinese companies amounted to US$ 65 billion in 2017, while sales of majority-owned foreign affiliates of American companies amounted to US$ 376 billion in the same year – there exists an imbalance of above US$ 300 billion. This is due to the significant difference of FDI stock between the two countries in their counterpart. Indeed, Chinese companies' investment in the United States is still in a very early stage – the size of their annual sales is only less than 8% of that of Japanese companies (US$ 835 billion in 2017). According to the latest data from China's Ministry of Commerce, the imbalance is larger, as sales of Chinese affiliates of American companies amounted to approximately US$ 700 billion. The large gap in data is due to difference in statistical scopes, as affiliates of minority ownership in joint ventures are counted in the Chinese case.

If we considered the three aspects – trade in goods, trade in services and sales of foreign affiliates (there is a bit overlap between latter two) – in a comprehensive manner, the picture of trade imbalance between China and the United States would be a very different one. In fact, this overall picture is the result of a long evolution of economic globalization, characterized by intensive economic interaction and reconfiguration after the end of the Cold War and especially since China's WTO accession. As part of the picture, the China–US imbalance in trade in goods is related to the patterns of a globalized production system. It is determined by the international division of labour and the distributional features of global value chains in the era of globalization. Therefore, a global perspective is crucial for a correct understanding of the nature and scale of China–US trade imbalance. It is part of the overall imbalance in the world economy, showing the need for a rebalancing effort at the global level, not only between China and the United States.

The trade imbalance between China and the United States is rooted in the supplementary features of their economies. Overall, there is a strong structural interdependence between the two economies, which has been formed and strengthened over the years of globalization. Institutional factors have largely contributed in this regard: the enhancing openness of the Chinese market has attracted growing investment of American companies, while the decreasing tariffs of both sides have fostered a rapid trade growth – especially in exports from China to the United States. In particular, China's WTO accession has led to significant reduction of Chinese tariffs on American imports, as the trade-weighted average tariff rate dropped from 18% in 2001 to 8% in 2005 (Figure 2.3). In fact, bilateral tariffs had already decreased in a very strong manner during the mid-1990s, contributing to the take-off of China–US trade. Since the mid-2000s, however, bilateral tariffs had remained at nearly the same level, and trade remedy measures of the United States against China rose significantly. In 2018 and 2019, bilateral tariffs started to surge due to the outbreak and escalation of the China–US trade war (Chapter 3, Section 3.1).

After the early 2000s, a "great leap forward" of Chinese exports took place, as China's WTO entry largely reduced policy uncertainty and promoted a large wave of foreign investment and production relocation from Western countries. The reduced uncertainty was related to changes in

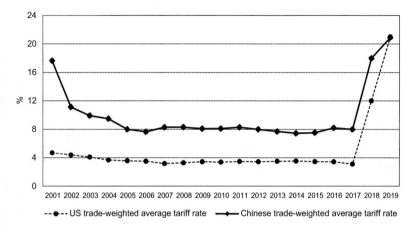

Figure 2.3 China–US bilateral tariff rates after China's WTO accession, 2001–2019
Source: Bown (2019).

China's domestic economic institutions and policies, as well as the general situation of the rule of law in China, especially in the (international) economic area. It was also reflected in other countries' trade policies, most importantly the abolishment of the obligatory annual review of China's MFN status by the US president and Congress. Empirical studies show that China's WTO accession contributed significantly to its export boom to the United States through a reduction in US trade policy uncertainty (Handley and Limão, 2017). Unfortunately, after being in the WTO for nearly two decades, China started to see a great degree of uncertainty brought back by high tariffs imposed during the China–US trade war (Chapter 3).

2.3 China–US rivalry: old and new means for solving disputes

The start of the China–US trade war in 2018 is not an accidental and isolated event, but accompanied by the continuous evolution of the global economic landscape, the significant adjustment of relations between the world's major powers, as well as considerable political and strategic changes that occurred in the United States. As an ancient Chinese proverb puts it: "no two rival tigers can exist in the same mountain". To some extent, it reflects intensified rivalry between the world's only incumbent superpower and an emerging "superpower", at least in the economic domain. It also reflects the emergence of a pivotal moment: the old mechanism for dispute settlement between the two countries does not work anymore, and the new ones are yet to come.

China has been rapidly rising for more than four decades, creating a development miracle based on both internal changes and external opportunities. Its great efforts in reform and opening up and its very proactive participation have made the country a main beneficiary of globalization. In 1980, China's GDP was US$ 300 billion, ranking eighth in the world and accounting for only one-tenth of that of the United States. In 2018, China's GDP reached US$ 14 trillion, about two-thirds of that of the United States. During the same period, China's GDP per capital rose from merely US$ 300 – one-fortieth of that of the United States – to US$ 10,000, or one-sixth of that of the US equivalent. Looking ahead, China's GDP is likely to surpass that of the United States, which has been the world's largest economy for more than a century. There is still great uncertainty as to when it will happen, but this will become a watershed in the world's economic history.

Over the past decade or so, China's industrial and technological upgrading has been advancing at a high speed. In recent years, Chinese companies have quickly moved up along the value chain, which are strongly supported by the policy initiatives of the Chinese government, such as the "Made in China 2025". From a political perspective, this has somehow weakened support from "Corporate America". The "friends" have not become "foes", but China's new advancement has severely challenged the dominance of US companies in technology, innovation and high value-added activities in such key industries as semiconductor and artificial intelligence. Furthermore, American companies have been facing increasing challenges within China, both from new government policies and stronger local competitors. China's economy (the world's second largest) and comprehensive national strength is still expanding rapidly, and so are its economic, military and political influences at the regional and global levels. In addition, the "superpower" in the making seems to have adopted a very different system, highlighting the potential competition with that of the United States.

In the face of various challenges from China, the voices calling for containing China have been continuously strengthened and have somehow gradually become a consensus in the United States. Many Americans believe that their country's goodwill and policy of engagement with China have not led to the expected results and have generally failed. As a result, the decades-long balance between engagement and containment needs to be broken. At the same time, the rising populism has provided the soil for the ascent of non-mainstream politics and the implementation of extreme policies. With the US government characterizing China as a "strategic competitor",[1] China–US relations have entered a new stage of intensified contradictions and rising uncertainties. The outbreak of the China–US trade war has become a manifestation of these.

The trade imbalance between China and the United States has existed for a long time (Figure 2.2). However, with the rapid narrowing of the economic gap between the two in recent years, the pressures brought by the "challenger" on the "defenders" have been increasing. Coupled with the rise of anti-globalization thoughts and the implementation of trade protectionist policies, the economic conflicts between China and the United States have intensified rapidly. This is rooted in the deep dissatisfaction of the United States with the status quo, which in turn comes from a serious reflection on history. Some Americans think that it was a mistake to let China join the WTO, and the US government has also experienced a change from being silent to being outspoken on this point. As early as in September 2010, Robert Lighthizer pointed out in his testimony to the China–US Economic Security Review Committee: the original intention of providing PNTR to China had not been realized; on the contrary, "Chinese mercantilism has had devastating effects on the U.S. economy".[2] Later, this rather radical judgement has become the "mainstream", as Mr. Lighthizer has been appointed as the US Trade Representative (USTR) within the Trump administration and become a key figure in the trade war against and related negotiations with China.

The paradigm shift of US trade policy and the use of unconventional means, such as trade wars, cannot be separated from the drastic changes in the US domestic political climate associated with rising populism. From the perspective of political economics, the negative impact of production offshoring on US manufacturing employment during the strong wave of globalization later contributed to the rise of the anti-globalization sentiment, trade protectionism and unilateralism. Despite significant welfare benefits, the PNTR led to the disappearance of a large number of manufacturing jobs (Pierce and Schott, 2016). From a longer period between 1990 and 2007, the impact of China's export growth accounted for about a quarter of the decrease in manufacturing employment in the United States (Autor et al., 2013). In the meantime, China's innovative capacity has been rapidly rising, and Chinese enterprises are rapidly upgrading to the high end of the value chain. This has weakened the voices of traditional supporters, especially those in the private sector.

Overall, status quo cannot be maintained. Changes taking place at both national and global levels, in both China and the United States, mean that it becomes almost impossible for the long-lasting pattern of the China–US economic relationship to be sustained. This pattern is characterized not only by the large and long-lasting imbalances in trade, but also by the significant and growing differences in the respective economic systems of China and the United States. From the perspective of China–US relations, the essence of the economic disagreement between the two countries lies in the fact that one side wants to change the status quo and the other wants to maintain it. Disputes over trade and economic interests are the key, and behind them lie diverging views about existing rules and institutions, as well as increasing clashes in economic systems and related governing principles.

Facing the mounting disputes, old means do not work anymore. Indeed, the pre-existing mechanism seems to be ineffective for solving the fundamental disagreement between China and the United States. In November 2016, Donald Trump was elected president of the United States, bringing the bilateral trade relations to the brink of a fundamental change. Unfortunately, the mechanism did not prevent a trade war from happening and become dysfunctional.

There has long been a bilateral dialogue mechanism between China and the United States, apart from the dispute settlement system at the multilateral level. In 2005, the China–US Strategic Dialogue was established. The following year, the China–US Strategic Economic Dialogue was launched. After six rounds of strategic dialogue and five rounds of strategic economic dialogue, the China–US Strategic and Economic Dialogue mechanism was established in 2009 to include both economic and security issues. A year later, the China–US High-Level Consultation on People-to-People Exchange mechanism was added. A framework of "G2" dialogue has been put in place. Through the mechanism of economic dialogues, concerns are expressed, pressures are presented, and solutions are discussed. Facing US pressure, for instance, China agreed to substantially appreciate its currency during 2005–2008, and it has also agreed at times to increase a certain amount of imports from the United States.

In April 2017, following the same approach started in 2005, the Chinese government and the Trump administration agreed to set up four high-level dialogue mechanisms covering diplomacy and security, economy, law enforcement and cyber security, and social exchanges. At the same time, the leaders of the two countries agreed to introduce a "100-Day Plan for China–US economic cooperation" to address trade imbalances between China and the United States. Accordingly, the two countries conducted a round of consultations from April to July 2017. However, no agreement had been reached on important issues. As a result, the first round of the newly introduced China–US Comprehensive Economic Dialogue, as one of the four mechanisms, held in Washington on 19 July failed to issue a joint statement.

Therefore, the decision makers in United States were disappointed to see that their previous efforts for adjusting the China–US economic relationship had not achieved the expected results. Then they decided to launch a

Section 301 investigation on China, the result of which led to the trade war between the two countries. It seems that China and the United States missed a rare window of opportunity to avoid such a trade war during the 100-Day Plan in 2017.

With regard to changing the status quo, it is natural that the US side is proactive, while the Chinese side seems to be passive. The former took the initiative to demand a big change in what it considered an unfair and unreasonable situation, while the latter has increasingly recognized that the status quo had to be adjusted. The question is what will be a "new status quo" acceptable to both sides. As an extreme scenario, a "decoupling" between the American and Chinese economies has been advocated by some people in the United States. It seems to make sense in theory, but it is unrealistic in practice. The main questions are how long it will take and how much costs both sides will have to pay.

To what extent the tariff increase will help solve the long-lasting problem of trade imbalances will depend on not only the imposed tariff itself, but also the result of the trade war – to what extent compromises are made to reduce the imbalances. Nevertheless, the sudden outbreak and rapid escalation of the China–US trade war demonstrates that the old equilibrium between the American and Chinese economies has been broken, and the results of the trade war and associated negotiations will determine a new balance between the world's two largest economies. It will be crucial to both of the countries and the world.

Notes

1 *National Security Strategy of the United States of America*, the White House, December 2017.
2 Robert E. Lighthizer, *Testimony before the U.S. China Economic and Security Review Commission: Evaluating China's Role in the World Trade Organization Over the Past Decade*, 9 June 2010.

3 The China–US trade war

Combat and compromise

> To fight and conquer in all your battles is not supreme excellence; to defeat the enemy without fighting is.
>
> – Sun Tzu

The China–US trade war showcases two intertwined processes of "fighting" and "talking", which are dealt with in the first two sections of the chapter respectively. The "war situation" has continuously evolved, highlighting the two aspects of "attack" and "counterattack". The United States instigated the trade war and has always been the party that took the initiative to attack, while, in response to the US provocation, China has retaliated with necessary countermeasures. In the meantime, a dynamic and intensive course of trade negotiations has involved high-level consultations and top leaders' interactions. Finally, trade diplomacy has led to a truce that prevents the further escalation of the trade war. Overall, the two countries have played an all-round, tit-for-tat game with a fascinating strategic and tactical dimension. Therefore, the last two sections of the chapter examine the China–US trade war from these angles.

3.1 The trigger of the trade war and the battle process

Since July 2018, China and the United States have been locked in a trade confrontation. By November 2019, a major part of the two sides' exports to each other had been placed under the "fire" of tariffs. On the side of China, exports subject to existing tariffs amounted to around US$ 360 billion, and some US$ 160 billion worth of goods would be tariffed in addition. On the side of the United States, affected exports were estimated at around US$ 120 billion – or about four-fifths of its total exports to China. Fortunately, trade talks made positive progress in October 2019, and the two sides signed an interim agreement for a "ceasefire" in January 2020.

It is worth noting that not all announced tariffs have been executed. The USTR has been implementing a tariff exclusion process. For instance, it has granted about US$ 3 billion in exemption tickets to favoured importers for the first round of tariffs valued at US$ 50 billion.[1] Similarly, China also excepted some types of US products in order to ease tensions during the negotiation process, for instance in September 2019, and particularly after the signing of the interim agreement.

The prelude

A Section 301 investigation launched by the US government against China was the prelude to the trade war. On 18 August 2017, the Office of the USTR initiated an investigation of China under Section 301 of the Trade Act of 1974 in response to a request by President Trump. The investigation aimed to examine "acts, policies, and practices of the Government of China related to technology transfer, intellectual property, and innovation".[2] A unilateral measure based on domestic legislation in the United States, the Section 301 investigation has been rarely used after the establishment of the WTO in 1995.

On 22 March 2018, USTR released the findings of the Section 301 investigation, stating that a series of Chinese actions are "unreasonable or discriminatory and burden or restrict U.S. commerce".[3] Accordingly, President Trump issued a Memorandum, lighting the fuse of a trade war. He requested 1) to consider increased tariffs on goods from China and publishing a proposed list of products and intended tariff increases; 2) to pursue dispute settlement in the WTO to address China's "discriminatory licensing practices"; and 3) to strengthen restrictions on Chinese investment in industries or technologies deemed important to the United States.[4]

Three phases of the trade war

Since the president of the United States fired the opening shot on 6 July 2018, the China–US trade war has experienced a series of escalations. Three major rounds of tariffs have mutually been imposed, and, thus, the trade war can be divided into three principal stages (Figure 3.1 and Appendix 1):

- *The first phase of the trade war broke out in July and August 2018.* This phase of the trade war involved the amount of exports valued at US$ 50 billion for both sides. On 3 April 2018, the United States announced a preliminary tariff list for Chinese goods worth US$ 50 billion. On the following day, the Chinese side also announced a list of the same amount. In the absence of concrete results from several rounds of

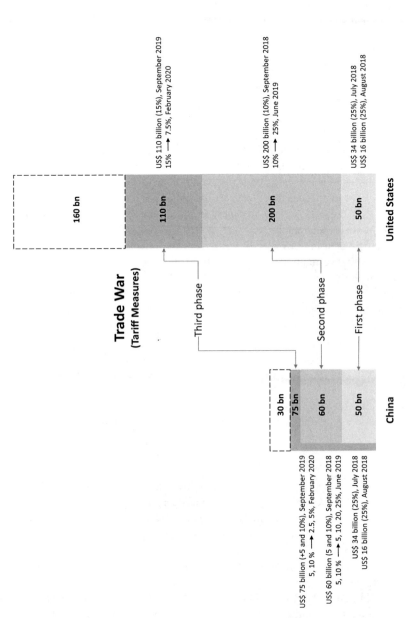

Figure 3.1 Three phases of the China–US trade war

negotiations in May (Section 3.2), the two sides announced their final tariff lists of US$ 50 billion on 15 and 16 June, respectively. The US list focused on China's high-end manufacturing products, such as mechanical, electrical and transport equipment, while the Chinese list covered agricultural, mineral and chemical products, automobiles and medical equipment. The implementation of tariffs was divided into two steps: on 6 July, the two sides began to impose a 25% tariff on imported products worth US$ 34 billion from each other, marking the outbreak of the China–US trade war; on 23 August, another US$ 16 billion worth of tariff measure came into effect.

- *The second phase of the trade war started in September 2018.* This phase of the trade war involved Chinese exports valued at US$ 200 billion to the United States and US$ 60 billion worth of American exports to China. On 10 July 2018, right after the beginning of the first round of the trade war, USTR announced a preliminary list of Chinese goods worth US$ 200 billion and started a related process of public hearing. On 2 August, the US side threatened that it would increase the tariff rate from 10% to 25%. On 3 August, the Chinese side released its list of American goods worth US$ 60 billion as a retaliation measure, with tariff rates set at 5%, 10%, 20% and 25%. On 17 September, the US side announced the final list of US$ 200 billion, to be implemented on 24 September 2018 with a tariff of 10%, which would be increased to 25% on 1 January 2019. The US list covered most industries and a very wide range of manufacturing products, and included some consumer products. The next day, China announced that it would impose tariffs of 5% or 10% on US$ 60 billion worth of US goods on the same date. The Chinese list extended to nearly all industries and product categories. On 24 September, the announced tariffs on products valued at US$ 200 billion and US$ 60 billion came into effect, respectively, and the second round of the trade war broke out.
- *After a temporary truce, the trade war escalated in June 2019.* After the onset of the second phase of the trade war, China and the United States took the opportunity of a bilateral summit to open an intensive negotiation process. At the working dinner on the occasion of the G20 Summit in Buenos Aires on 1 December, the leaders of the two countries decided to suspend the escalation of tariffs. The two sides decided to conduct a 90-day negotiation. Accordingly, the US administration announced a postponement of the date, initially planned on 1 January 2019, to increase the tariff on Chinese products worth US$ 200 billion from 10% to 25%. The new date was set to 1 March 2019. After passing the deadline at the end of February, the negotiations continued and the planned tariff increase was further postponed, without a new deadline

specified. However, in early May, the negotiations derailed. The US side immediately announced on 9 May that it would raise the tariff of goods worth US$ 200 billion to 25%. On 13 May, the Chinese side announced a countermeasure to raise the tariff rate of goods valued at US$ 60 billion by a range of four levels (5, 10, 20 and 25%). The US side set the tariff effective date on 1 June and then postponed it till 15 June.

- *The third phase of trade war broke out in September 2019.* This phase of the trade war involved about US$ 300 billion Chinese worth of exports to the United States and American exports valued at US$ 75 billion to China. For the former, the products included in the goods worth US$ 300 billion are additional, while for the latter, most are duplicates of goods cited in the earlier rounds of tariff lists. At the end of July 2019, a new round of negotiations in Shanghai went into a deadlock. On 1 August, therefore, President Trump announced a levy of 10% of tariff on all remaining Chinese imports amounting to about US$ 300 billion. On 13 August, the United States announced that the tariff would be implemented first on Chinese goods worth US$ 110 billion on 1 September and then on Chinese goods worth US$ 160 billion on 15 December. On 23 August, China announced its countermeasure, adding 5% or 10% of tariffs to US$ 75 billion worth of US goods. In the meantime, China announced that tariffs would be resumed on US automobiles and auto parts, which had been suspended since 1 January 2019. Subsequently, President Trump immediately announced retaliatory measures, imposing an additional 5% tariff on all Chinese imports. On 1 September, the first part of the third phase of the tariffs came into effect: United States imposed a 15% tariff on Chinese goods valued at US$ 112 billion; China added 5% or 10% tariffs to about 1,700 different US goods.

- *Phase One trade agreement stopped further escalation of the trade war.* Reached on 13 December 2019, the Phase One trade deal between China and the United States realized a ceasefire. The US side agreed not to impose tariffs on US$ 160 billion worth of Chinese imports planned on 15 December. In addition, the tariff rate on "approximately US$ 120 billion" of Chinese imports would be reduced from 15% to 7.5%. Therefore, a major part of the third round of the trade war has been reversed. However, the United States will be maintaining its 25% tariffs on US$ 250 billion worth of Chinese imports, imposed during the first and second phases of the trade war.

Due to the China–US trade war, bilateral tariffs surged (Figure 3.2). Through three phases of tariff measures, both sides have drastically increased their overall levels of tariffs on imports from the other side. The trade-weighted average of Chinese tariffs on US imports has already increased

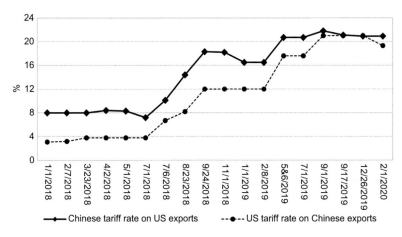

Figure 3.2 China–US bilateral tariff rates after the outbreak of trade war
Source: Bown (2019).

beyond the pre-WTO level, while the US equivalent has risen three-fold that in the early 2000s – a level similar to that in the early 1930s.

Trade or technology war?

During the process of the trade war against China, the United States has also used various means beyond tariffs. It has introduced several restrictive measures against Chinese technology companies in order to prevent them from entering the US markets on the one hand, and to limit their access to US components on the other hand. For the latter, the US government does so primarily through implementing the Entity List,[5] which is a supplementary document to the "Export Administration Regulations" governed by the Industry and Security Bureau of the US Department of Commerce. Major measures against Chinese enterprises during the trade war include the seven-year export ban for ZTE announced in April 2018 (cancelled in July 2018), the inclusion in the Entity List of Huawei Technology and its subsidiaries in May 2019 of five Chinese companies engaged in supercomputing in June 2019 and of eight Chinese companies in artificial intelligence (AI) business in August 2019 (Appendix 2). In early 2020, the Commerce Department took measures to restrict exports of artificial intelligence software as a renewed effort to keep advanced technologies out of the hands of rival powers like China.

The United States has also tried to prevent foreign companies from selling advanced equipment to China. The country can require a license if US-made components make up more than 25% of the value. In the case of ASML of the Netherlands, its sales of extreme ultraviolet lithography (EUV) machine to China had received a licence from the Dutch government but was later blocked by the US administration. The US Department of Commerce found that ASML's EUV machine did not meet the 25% threshold. Therefore, the government agency has started to consider lowering the threshold for specific cases. In late 2018 and early 2019, the US government started to press the Dutch government on security basis, as lithography equipment falls under the purview of the Wassenaar Arrangement, which coordinates export restrictions of "dual-use" technology that has both commercial and military applications.[6]

It seems that the United States has launched "a technology cold war" against China, targeting key sectors such as 5G telecom, semiconductor, supercomputing and AI. Indeed, Huawei and ZTE, two major Chinese telecom equipment manufacturers, have become major targets of the US actions during the trade war. On 1 December 2018, Ms. Meng Wanzhou, the CFO of the Huawei, was arrested in Canada upon a US request for her extradition. In January 2019, the United States unveiled a criminal charge against Huawei, and, later in March, Huawei sued the US government over the ban on its products in the United Sates. In May 2019, differences between China and the United States on key issues during the trade negotiations have intensified. On this basis, the United States had a drastic reaction to the tariff escalation and dealt Huawei, the pearl in the crown of China's high-tech industry, a painful hand. Facing various US sanctions, Huawei had to abandon American markets and reduce its sourcing from American companies. However, this has not had much effect on the company's overall performance. In the first three quarters of 2019, its global revenues rose by 24% to RMB¥ 611 billion (or US$ 89 billion). By October 2019, Huawei has signed more than 60 commercial contracts for 5G networks worldwide. The US offensive continued: in February 2020, the US government charged Huawei and two of its subsidiaries with federal racketeering and conspiracy to steal trade secrets from American companies (Appendix 2).

The focus of the Section 301 investigation launched in August 2017, which provoked the China–US trade war, is on China's laws, policies and practices related to intellectual property, innovation and technology. The concern of the US government is whether these Chinese laws, policies and practices may "encourage or require the transfer of American technology and intellectual property to enterprises in China", "negatively affect American economic interests", or "be harming American intellectual property rights, innovation, or technology development".[7] However, behind these concerns is the intensified technological rivalry between China and the United States, which leads to worries about China's technological drive and its implication for the US leadership. In the findings of the Section 301 investigation, the USTR lists a number of China's industrial policies, especially "Made in China 2025" introduced in 2015. As China's ten-year plan for targeting ten advanced technology industries, it sets out explicit market share targets and showcases strong government support.

At the same time, with the escalation of the trade war, potential conflicts in the financial area have begun to emerge. On 25 June 2019, three Chinese banks were ruled by US judges to refuse to comply with relevant subpoenas and may therefore be denied access to the US financial system. More important is the disagreement between China and the United States around the exchange rate. On 5 August 2019, the US Treasury designated China as a "currency manipulator", immediately after the People's Bank of China allowed the Chinese currency RMB to depreciate against the US dollar surpassing the key psychological level of 7. Due to the sensitivity of exchange rates for the bilateral economic relationship, it continues to be one of the major issues in trade talks between China and the United States.

3.2 The negotiations and an interim agreement

The trade war has unfolded in parallel with an intensive process of negotiations between two teams of high-level government officials. The US team is led by Trade Representative Robert Lighthizer and Treasury Secretary Steven Mnuchin, with the involvement of other very important officials and a range of federal government agencies, including the Office of the USTR, the Treasury Department, the Commerce Department, the Agriculture Department, the Energy Department, the State Department and relevant bodies of the White House. On the Chinese side, the negotiation team is headed by Vice Premier Liu He, who oversees major economic affairs within the Chinese government. The Chinese negotiation team involves minister- or vice-minister-level officials from various government agencies, including the People's Bank of China, the Ministry of Finance, the Ministry of Commerce, the Ministry of Agriculture and Rural Affairs, the National Development and Reform Commission, the Ministry of Industry and Information Technology and the Minister of Foreign Affairs. By November 2019, the two sides had held 13 rounds of so-called "China–US High-level Economic and Trade Consultations" (hereafter referred to as "economic and trade consultations") – defined and counted by the Chinese side (Appendix 1), which at the end led to the Phase One trade agreement.

Major rounds of trade negotiation

Since the beginning of the trade war, China–US negotiations have experienced twists and turns. The economic and trade consultations started with Vice Premier Liu He's visit to the United States during 27 February–3 March

2018. By November 2019, there had been three major waves of negotiation: the first one during May–June 2018 (Rounds 2–4 of economic and trade consultations), the second one during January–May 2019 (Rounds 5–11) and the third one during July and October 2019 (Rounds 12 and 13). The location of economic and trade consultations rotates between Beijing and Washington. There have been some major rounds of vice-ministerial-level consultations, while others took place for preparing the high-level consultations (Appendix Table 1). In addition, there were two major summits, which played a critical role in the overall negotiation process:

- *Negotiations in May 2018 did not prevent the trade war from occurring.* After the signing of the Presidential Memorandum in March 2018 and the announcement of the US\$ 50 billion tariff lists in the month after, China and the United States held three rounds of economic and trade consultations in May and early June. On 15 May, as the Special Envoy of President Xi Jinping, Vice Premier Liu He led a delegation to visit the United States and meet with major members of the American negotiation team, including USTR Robert Lighthizer, Treasury Secretary Steven Mnuchin and Commerce Secretary Wilbur Ross. On 19 May, the two sides issued a joint statement, saying that they would take effective measures to substantially reduce the US trade deficit with China.[8] Ten days later, however, the White House said that the United States would release the final US\$ 50 billion list of products in June for a 25% tariff, continue WTO dispute settlement against China originally initiated in March, and implement specific investment restrictions and enhanced export controls towards China.[9] On 15 June, the list was announced as scheduled, and the China–US trade war broke out in the following month. Obviously, the three rounds of key consultations in May and early June did not manage to prevent the trade war, as the stance of the US side remained tough. Overall, China thought that the United States asked too much and the United States thought that China lacked flexibility.
- *A summit on 1 December 2018 agreed on a temporary ceasefire.* After the outbreak of a trade war in July and subsequent escalation in September, a bilateral meeting at the G20 Summit in Buenos Aires on 1 December provided an opportunity for the Chinese and Americans to talk with each other. During a working dinner, the heads of state of China and the United States decided to stop upgrading trade restriction measures and set out to resolve mutual concerns. However, the two sides did not issue a joint statement, and the different interpretations of the outcome of the talks indicated that the subsequent trade negotiations still faced enormous challenges. The first is the challenge of negotiating contents,

especially regarding "structural changes" of the Chinese economy. The US statement said that President Trump and President Xi had agreed to "immediately begin negotiations on structural changes with respect to forced technology transfer, intellectual property protection, non-tariff barriers, cyber intrusions and cyber theft, services and agriculture". The second challenge is time limitation. According to the US side, both parties agreed to "have this transaction completed within the next 90 days".[10] If they are unable to reach an agreement, the 10% tariffs will be raised to 25%. Obviously, the US side continued its strong pressure.

- *Intensive negotiations from January to April 2019.* The summit in December 2018 kicked off a wave of intensive trade talk. It is not easy for the two sides to shift their consensus from "dining table" to "negotiation table", but the two leaders' agreement had provided strong momentum and guidance for the trade negotiations. The Chinese side reported positive progresses after the subsequent rounds of consultations. In the 6th round of Economic and Trade Consultation held in Beijing on 14–15 February 2019, the two sides reached a principled consensus on the main issues of the negotiations. During the 7th round held in Washington on 21–24 February, they made substantial progress on these issues. Considering this progress, President Trump announced on 25 February that he would postpone the scheduled increase in tariffs, without setting a new deadline. During the 8th round consultation held on 28–29 March, the two sides discussed the text of a seemingly upcoming agreement. The 9th round consultation from 3–5 April made new progress regarding "texts on technology transfer, intellectual property protection, non-tariff measures, services, agriculture, trade balance and implementation mechanisms",[11] and the two sides decided to talk about the remaining issues in the next stage. From 30 April to 1 May, the 10th round of consultations was held in Beijing. This time, the Chinese side did not announce specific results, but the US side said that the negotiations were "fruitful".

- *A major setback in early May and an uncertain compromise in late June 2019.* After receiving China's amendment to the negotiated text of the agreement in early May, the US side had a strong reaction. On the 9th of the month, the USTR announced to increase tariffs. On the same date, the Chinese delegation arrived in the United States for the previously planned 11th round of economic and trade consultations. However, the size of the delegation, scheduled to be more than 100 people, had been substantially reduced. Vice Premier Liu He held a media interview, saying that the consultations had not broken down, but the two sides had differences in three main aspects: whether to abolish all tariff increases, the scale of trade purchases and the balance of the text.

He emphasized that China would never give in on the issues of principle. After the United States introduced a series of harsh measures, including those against Huawei, China adopted some countermeasures, including the increase of the US$ 60 billion tariffs and the establishment of an "unreliable entity list" system. The trust between the two sides had been damaged and the uncertainty of negotiations had largely increased. At a crucial moment, the leaders of the two countries met on 29 June during the G20 Osaka Summit. They agreed to resume economic and trade consultations. According to the Chinese account, the US side stated that it would not impose new tariffs on Chinese exports. In addition, President Trump also mentioned that US companies would be allowed to continue to supply to Huawei.

- *The U turn between two rounds of consultations.* To follow up with the leaders' decision in Osaka, the two negotiation teams held the 12th round of economic and trade consultations on 30–31 July 2019. For the first time, consultations took place in Shanghai, a symbolic location where the historic Joint Communiqué of the United States and China was issued in 1972. However, positions of the two sides basically remained unchanged and they failed to reach an agreement on China's massive purchase of US agricultural products. The failure of this round of consultations led to a serious escalation of the trade war in August. In September, China and the United States began to ease their confrontational stances. President Trump announced that the tariff increase originally scheduled for 1 October (the National Day of China) was postponed until 15 October. Chinese companies also began to purchase US agricultural products. On 19 September, Vice Minister of Finance Liao Min led a delegation to visit the United States and conducted a working level dialogue. On 10 October, Vice Premier Liu He arrived in Washington for the 13th round of economic and trade consultations. The talks have made substantial progress, laying a foundation for the signing of the interim agreement.

Phase One trade agreement and the upcoming Phase Two negotiations

In normal negotiations, nothing is agreed until everything is agreed. However, China and the United States could not wait until everything is agreed. On 15 January 2020, President Trump and Vice Premier Liu signed an Economic and Trade Agreement, which is regarded as the Phase One agreement between the two countries. Already announced on 13 December, the Phase One trade deal requires substantial structural reforms and other changes to China's economic and trade regime in the areas of intellectual property, technology transfer, agriculture, financial services, and currency and foreign exchange, and it also includes commitments from China to make substantial additional purchases of American goods and services. In exchange, the United States has agreed to modify its Section 301 tariff actions. It will maintain 25% tariffs on US$ 250 billion worth of Chinese imports, but a reduced tariff rate from 15% to 7.5% on "approximately US$ 120 billion" worth of Chinese imports.

The Phase One agreement is not a typical trade agreement aiming at promoting free trade. China's commitment to structural reforms is in line with the US requests and the consensus reached on 1 December 2018. More importantly, the Expanding Trade chapter of the agreement contains China's commitment to import various US goods and services during 2020 and 2021 in a total amount that exceeds China's annual level of imports for those goods and services in 2017 by no less than US$ 200 billion (Appendix 3). The chapter also contains a secret annex of product-by-product commitments, through which China promises to import certain amounts or volumes of detailed goods and services, regardless of market prices or demand conditions – the only way to fulfil these commitments is to resort to "managed trade".[12] In order to facilitate its promised purchases, China started to offer tariff exemption to a large number of US products after the Phase One agreement became effective on 14 February 2020. Therefore, an actual outcome of the agreement is that Chinese tariffs drop while US tariffs persist.

The implementation of the Phase One agreement will have significant implications for the American and Chinese economies as well as some third party countries. Overall, the growth of the US economy will be boosted by a significant amount of additional demand from China – an estimated 0.5 percentage point per year during 2020 and 2021. By contrast, the Chinese economy may face downward pressures due to the huge promised purchases, and the economic consequences of the COVID-19 pandemic would make them more difficult to implement. Specific third party countries, which export products like export oil and gas, agricultural products and aircrafts to China, may suffer from potential trade diversions.

The Phase One deal is somehow a "ceasefire" agreement between China and the United States. Apart from what was written in the agreement, the US side has also agreed to remove China from the list of "currency manipulators" and to resume the Comprehensive Economic Dialogue, which would go in parallel with the trade negotiation process. Though a relatively small part of the imposed tariffs would be rolled back accordingly, it was a crucial start. Thus, the agreement can be considered as a steppingstone to a final deal to end the China–US trade war and a key turning point in the evolution of the trade talks between the two sides. However, several economies have expressed their concerns about the agreement's compliance with WTO principles, particularly the non-discrimination principle of MFN, and its potential distortion of trade flows.

The Phase Two negotiations will not be an easy task, and their prospects are uncertain. Both China and the United States must make some "basic adjustments" to reach a lasting trade deal that benefits the rest of the world.[13] Important questions are: 1) Will they be able to finally remove all existing tariffs and accordingly end the trade war? 2) Will there be a breakthrough in major issues, such as industrial subsidies? 3) Will China be able to promise significant purchases of American goods and services for the years after 2021? and 4) How will the implementation of the Phase One agreement, which might be affected by the COVID-19 pandemic, influence the Phase Two negotiations?

The issue of industrial subsidies is not covered in the Phase One agreement between the United States and China, but the latter continues to feel the pressure at the multilateral level. Published on 14 January 2020, the 7th Joint Statement of the Trilateral Meeting of the Trade Ministers of Japan, the United States and the European Union focuses on the WTO's Agreement on Subsidies and Countervailing Measures. The agreed direction of amending relevant articles of this agreement points to a fundamental change of international rules on industrial subsidies, which will have a significant implication for China's current policy practices. In this area, the Chinese "bottom line" is not only a matter of bilateral economic and trade relations, but also a choice of its future development model – this would be a major challenge in the upcoming negotiations. Therefore, the overall prospects of the China–US trade war remain uncertain.

3.3 Game perspective

By applying the game theory on general trade wars to the specific China–US case, we can have a deeper understanding of its interactive nature and strategic characteristics. Different game theoretical approaches – static and dynamic games, simultaneous and sequential games – reflect different aspects of the decision making of the two involved parties. We use static game, finite repeated game and infinite repeated game to illustrate the interaction between China and the United States during the trade war. Following the assumptions made in the theoretical discussion (Chapter 1, Section 1.3), we focus on trade and use the real export loss to calculate payoffs and depict the payoff matrix accordingly.

Static game

Tariff pass-through is normally incomplete. When the United States imposes special tariffs on Chinese goods, Chinese exporters tend to lower the pre-tax prices of export commodities in order to maintain the market in the United States. The increase of after-tax price that American consumers bear is thus less than the tariffs charged by the government, which imply that the extra tariff is shared by Chinese exporters and the consumers in the United States. Assume that the tariff pass-through rate of China is 20%, and the price elasticity of demand for exports is 4; the tariff pass-through rate of the United States is also 20%, and the price elasticity of demand for exports is 3. In the China–US trade war, both China and the United States are major importing countries for each other, so we assume that imposing tariff has a positive impact on the national welfare of both countries and the benefit is 1% of its initial imports volume.

As of February 2020, the United States had imposed tariffs that range from 7.5% to 25% on around US\$ 370 billion worth of Chinese exports,[14] and China had imposed tariffs ranging from 5% to 25% on US\$ 120 billion worth of American exports.[15] It is estimated that the United States imposes an average tariff of 19.3% tariff on US\$ 370 billion worth of Chinese goods and China imposes an average tariff of 18.5% tariff on US\$ 120 billion worth of Chinese goods. We assume that China and the United States have two actions, that is, to impose tariffs and not to impose tariffs, and the payoffs of both countries are 0 prior to imposing tariffs. The payoff can be calculated (as discussed in Chapter 1, Section 1.3), with the payoff matrix depicted. Based on the previously mentioned assumption of tariff pass-through rates, the influence of US tariffs on the overall price of Chinese exports to the United States would be 19.3% × 20% = 3.86%. As the supposed price elasticity is 4, the demand for exports changes by 3.86% × 4 = 15.44%. Therefore, the number of Chinese exports to the United States changes by (1 − 15.44%) × (1 + 3.86%) − 1 = −12.176%, that is, Chinese exports to the United States will decrease by 12.176%. Accordingly, if the United States imposes tariffs on China and China does not retaliate, then the payoff of China is US\$ 370 × (−12.176%) ≈ −45.05 billion. Other calculations are similar, and the payoff matrix is as follows:

The China–US trade war		China	
		Not to impose tariff	To impose tariff
United States	Not to impose tariff	(0, 0)	(−9.37, 1.2)
	To impose tariff	(3.7, −45.05)	(−5.67, −43.85)

The Nash Equilibrium is a strategy profile with payoffs (−5.67, −43.85), meaning both countries choose to impose tariffs. Looking into the reality of the China–US trade war, the economic goal of the United States is to maximize national welfare, reduce the China–US trade deficit and require specific structural changes to the Chinese economy. The country is willing to sacrifice short-term interests for its long-term benefits. On the other hand, China's goal is generally to make the smallest possible concessions. It is ready to retaliate in order to protect its strategic interests in the long run. Thus, the export aspect depicted in the payoff matrix is only one dimension in the strategic interaction between the two countries during the trade war, and the decision making in the China–US trade war is much more complicated.

Finite repeated game

Based on the same assumptions on the tariff pass-through rate, the price elasticity of demand for exports and the welfare gains from imposing tariffs, we develop the model of a finite repeated game. The model incorporates the gradual and dynamic nature of the strategic interaction between China and the United States during the three phases of the trade war. It helps predict the outcome, though a sequential game would better capture the interactive nature of the trade war and its gradual escalation.

During the first phase of the trade war, the United States imposed 25% tariffs on 1,300 separate tariff items involving US$ 50 billion. China announced 25% tariff on US$ 50 billion imports from the United States. We assume that China and the United States have two actions, that is, to impose tariffs and not to impose tariffs, and the payoff of both countries is 0 prior to imposing tariffs. The payoff in other situations can be calculated as per the calculation in Section 1.1. For instance, the price of US goods would change by 25% × 20% = 5% approximately. As the price elasticity of demand for exports is 3, the demand for exports would drop by about 5% × 3 = 15%. Then the US exports to the China will change by $(1 - 15\%) \times (1 + 5\%) - 1 = -15.75\%$, that is, if China imposes extra tariffs on the United States but the United States does not impose extra tariffs on China, then the payoff of the United States is 50 × (−15.75%) ≈ −7.88 billion. Other calculations are similar and therefore, the payoff matrix in the first stage is assumed as follows.

1. First phase of the trade war		**China**	
		Not to impose tariff	To impose tariff
United States	Not to impose tariff	(0, 0)	(−7.88, 0.5)
	To impose tariff	(0.5, −8)	(−7.38, −7.5)

During the second phase of the trade war, the United States announced the imposition of a 10% import tariff on 5,745 items valued at approximately US$ 200 billion originating from China. Consequently, China announced an additional 10% and 5% tariff on US$ 60 billion worth of imported products. Assume that the payoff of both countries is 0 prior to imposing tariffs again. Similarly, the payoff matrix can be calculated as follows according to the calculation in Section 1.1.

2. Second phase of the trade war		China	
		Not to impose tariff	To impose tariff
United States	Not to impose tariff	(0, 0)	(−1.84, 0.6)
	To impose tariff	(2, −12.32)	(0.16, −11.72)

The second phase of the trade war escalated. As a result, the United States announced that the tariff rate on US$ 200 billion worth of goods imported from China would increase from 10% to 25%, and China announced that the tariffs would increase again by 15%, 10% or 5% for US goods valued at US$ 60 billion. Assume that the payoff of both countries is 0 prior to imposing tariffs again. Similarly, the payoff matrix can be calculated as follows.

3. Escalation of the second phase of the trade war		China	
		Not to impose tariff	To impose tariff
United States	Not to impose tariff	(0, 0)	(−2.47, 0.6)
	To impose tariff	(2, −18.72)	(−0.47, −18.12)

During the third phase of the trade war, the United States imposed a 15% tariff on all remaining Chinese goods worth approximately US$ 125 billion. China announced its decision to impose tariffs ranging from 5% to 10% on imported goods originating from the United States with 5,078 taxable items worth approximately US$ 76 billion. Later, the United States cut tariffs on US$ 120 billion worth of goods from China to 7.5%. Up to now, China only imposes tariffs on the part of the goods that are listed in the 5,078 taxable items, which is estimated at about US$ 10 billion. Assume that the payoff of both countries is 0 prior to imposing tariffs again. Similarly, the payoff matrix can be calculated as follows.

4. Third phase of the trade war		China	
		Not to impose tariff	To impose tariff
United States	Not to impose tariff	(0, 0)	(−0.31, 0.1)
	To impose tariff	(1.2, −5.51)	(0.89, −5.41)

Considering the fourth stage of the game first, both players would choose "impose tariff" based on backward induction. In the third stage, rational players are aware that regardless of the outcome at this stage, the outcome of the fourth stage is (0.89, −5.4). Thus, both players would still choose to impose tariffs in the third stage. Similarly, in the first and second stages, both players choose to impose tariffs. Therefore, in the finite dynamic game with complete information, both countries consistently choose to impose tariffs.

Infinite repeated game

We assume that the game of the China–US trade war is played over the infinite horizon, and the payoff matrix at each stage of the trade war is the same. In this case, a one-off game (also called the stage game) repeats infinitely. Assume that there exists a trigger strategy, through which both players attempt to cooperate initially and once they find that the other player fails to cooperate, they will subsequently adopt a non-cooperative strategy to retaliate and do so forever. This may lead to a subgame perfect Nash Equilibrium[16] that benefits both players. With regard to the China–US trade war, assume the payoff matrix of the one-off game is the same as the payoff matrix in the static game discussed earlier.

Suppose that China adopts the trigger strategy and the discount factor is δ. The discount factor indicates the discount of utility, which is related to the participant's time preference. This factor can be understood as the participant's patience level. The value range is [0, 1]. A large discount factor indicates the participants' high level of patience. If the payoff in the t stage of the infinite repeated game is "a", the present value of the payoff in the t stage is "$\delta^{t-1} \times a$". Generally, when the discount factor δ reaches a certain level, the best strategy of the United States is also the trigger strategy.

In the first phase of the trade war, the United States can choose whether to impose tariffs or not. If the country imposes tariffs, its payoff in the first stage is 3.7, then because of the trigger strategy, China will likewise impose tariffs from the next stage to retaliate. In order to maximize its gains, the United States would also impose tariffs from the next stage, which means that the payoff would constantly be -5.67. Assume that the present value of the total payoff of the United States in the situation is ω. Thus, the present value of the total payoff of the United States could be calculated as follows:

$$\omega = 3.7 - 5.672 \times \delta - 5.672 \times \delta^2 - \ldots = 3.7 - 5.672 \times \frac{\delta}{1-\delta}$$

If the United States does not impose tariffs in the first phase, the payoff is 0. In the next stage, the United States will face the same choice. Let V stand for the present value of the total payoff of the United States in this situation, V_1 stands for the total payoff from the second stage of the infinite repeated game, then the present value of the payoff starting from the second stage is $\delta \times V_1$. Thus, the total payoff of the United States in the entire infinite repeated game is:

$$V = 0 + \delta \times V_1$$

Because the payoff in the first stage is 0, $V = V_1$. Thus, we know that $V = 0$. If $V > \omega$, the United States would choose not to impose tariffs, which represents a cooperation strategy. Specifically, when $0 > 3.7 - 5.672 \times \frac{\delta}{1-\delta}$, that is, $\delta > 0.4$, the United States will choose to cooperate in the first stage. The infinite repeated game for the later stages is similar. Therefore, the optimal choice for the United States is to adopt the same trigger strategy to China. Likewise, the optimal choice for China is to adopt the same trigger strategy when $\delta > 0.4$. Given that the subgames of the infinite repeated game remain the same, the trigger strategy applies in all of them. The combination of the trigger strategy constitutes a subgame perfect Nash Equilibrium of the entire infinite repeated game of the China–US trade war.

In this trigger strategy equilibrium, once a player accidently deviates from the equilibrium path, both players end up with imposing tariffs. Does there exist an equilibrium in which players go back to play the cooperative strategy even after someone deviates? The answer is yes. We can construct an equilibrium with limited punishment and forgiveness. Consider the following strategy profile: each player starts with the cooperative strategy and will continue to cooperate if no one defects. If one player defects, then each player will choose defection for k periods. After k periods of punishment, each player will go back to the cooperative path. It is not difficult to show that when k and δ satisfy certain conditions, the earlier strategy profile constitutes a subgame perfect equilibrium. Just like what happened during the China–US trade war, after several rounds of tariffs and retaliations, both sides tend to cooperate.

3.4 Strategic dimension

Since participants do not choose to play out their cards at one time, trade wars often involve dynamic games (Section 3.3). In the real world of trade confrontation, there are two interrelated interactive processes of "fighting" and "talking". In case Country A makes a request and expects to obtain concessions from country B by giving pressures, the latter can choose to refuse completely, meet the requirements unconditionally, or make partial or conditional concessions through negotiation. If Country B chooses to negotiate, then there appears a round of "threat-negotiation" process. If the negotiation fails, Country B refuses requests of Country A or the compromise is not sufficient, then Country A may choose to impose tariffs. At this point, Country B can choose not to act and continue the talks or take countermeasures. If the latter is chosen, a round of "attack-counterattack" process will take place. These two interactive processes may alternate, thus leading to the dynamic process of an escalating trade war and continuing trade negotiations.

Countries face a range of strategic and/or tactical issues during their trade confrontation. With regard to the tariff war, the two participating countries have plenty of flexibility in deciding the scope and strength of their tariff measures, as they can choose not only a specific group of products with a certain amount of trade volume but also a specific level of special tariffs. They can start with a rather constrained measure and upgrade it in terms of the scope of products and the level of tariffs. In addition, they can expand their actions beyond tariffs. Like in a war, there are two interrelated aspects of "offense" and "defense". The offensive ability of a country in a pure tariff war depends on its ability to impose special tariffs, the scale of which depends on taxable imports from the counterpart. Its defensive ability depends on the economy's resilience to tariffs imposed by the other party, which is reflected in export performance, as well as in the overall reaction of enterprises, industries, macroeconomy and financial markets (Chapter 4). The (relative) economic impacts on both sides will affect the realization of political goals of the trade war and may also lead to changes in judgements and stances of the two sides in the negotiation process.

The trade between China and the United States is highly unbalanced (Chapter 2, Section 2.2), and so is the "arsenal" of tariffs between the two countries. This results in an unbalanced trade warfare. In other words, a total of more than US$ 500 billion worth of China's exports to the United States can be targeted by US tariffs, while China's imports from the United

States, which can be targeted by Chinese tariffs, are less than one-thirds of that amount. From the point of view of trade negotiations, the part of exports that has become subject to tariffs will continue to negatively affect domestic economy, while the part of exports that has not yet been subject to tariffs may be subject to threats from the other party, both of which will bring pressures on negotiators. This partly explains why the US side takes the lead in the trade war as well as negotiation.

During the China–US trade war, the strategy of the US side demonstrates the following characteristics:

- *Maximum pressure.* From the beginning, the US side puts forward a very high demand and pursues a "winner takes all" outcome. In order to get the maximal concession, it uses strong tariff measures as a threat during the negotiations. When the negotiation result is not satisfactory, the tariff measure is implemented as a punishment for the counterpart's tough stance in the previous round of negotiations and as a pressure to facilitate the next round of negotiations. During the China–US trade war, the US side has made full use of its advantages, including a large "arsenal" of tariff measures, a well-performing domestic economy, and its strong resilience to external pressures. Overall it has adopted a very tough stance and harsh measures in order to exert "maximum pressure" on China.
- *Gradual escalation.* The US side adopts a gradualist approach, playing its cards one by one. Tariff measures have been gradually upgraded regarding both the scale of commodities (from US$ 50 billion to US$ 200 billion, and then to the threat of US$ 300 billion) and the level of tariffs (from 10% to 25%, and then to the threat of further upgrading). In addition, the US side expanded tariff measures from industrial goods to consumer goods, and it started with a group of products (US$ 50 billion) that China accounted for as a relatively small share of its imports. By doing so, the economic impact of tariffs can be observed and controlled, and follow-up measures can be retained in the negotiations.
- *Comprehensive offense.* The US side uses a wide range of offensive measures apart from special tariffs. In particular, it adopts repressive measures against key Chinese enterprises to force the Chinese side to compromise. For example, the US sanctions against Chinese enterprises ZTE and Huawei were all launched at critical moments during trade negotiations, with the obvious intention of boosting the "trade war" through a "technology war".

The China–US trade war should be seen in the context of the ongoing restructuring of the global trading system. As a party dissatisfied with the status quo and trying to change it, the United States has been leading this restructuring, while major economies including China, the European Union and Japan are the main players. This involves the reform of the multilateral trading system with the WTO as its core, the revision and initiation of major free trade negotiations for the United States and threatening or resorting to trade war in order to maximize the US interests. In terms of the second aspect, a clear negotiation sequence and priority level have been determined, starting with North America, its backyard, and expanding to major developed economics, such as the European Union and Japan. Behind the well concerted actions at the bilateral, regional and multilateral levels, a grand strategy seems to exist with the aim to construct a new global trade order led by the United States and beneficial to the United States.

Fighting a trade war with China seems to be an important part of such a strategy. The trade team of the Trump administration focuses on the bilateral level, through which it can most leverage the country's strengths in trade talks so as to maximize US interests. With regard to trade disputes and frictions, they do not put their efforts within the framework of multilateral rules but take unilateral actions. They do not hesitate to use or threaten to use tariff measures to wage a trade war. The United States has made threats to many trading partners, but avoided fighting with them simultaneously. It has picked up China as the main target. The United States has a huge deficit with China, which is much higher than those of other trading partners; at the same time, the rivalry with China in fields such as science and technology has intensified (Chapter 2). This explains why the United States has chosen to take on China on trade issues and to concentrate its "firepower" of tariffs against China, while deciding to settle with the European Union and Japan and start free trade negotiations with them.

The trade warfare with China may have been masterminded by an experienced "trade warrior" – USTR Robert Lighthizer. Another leader of the US negotiation team is the Treasury Secretary Steven Mnuchin. In the early rounds of economic and trade consultations, Wilbur Ross (Commerce Secretary), Larry Kudlow (Director of National Economic Council) and Peter Navarro (Assistant to the President and Director of the Office of Trade and Manufacturing Policy) were also involved. The co-existence of both "hawks" and "doves" provides flexibility for making necessary adjustments during the negotiations. At the same time, the president dominates the negotiation process from the top, announcing many major decisions through his Twitter, which is in line with an overall new approach of communication between the administration and the outside world.

The "Head of State Diplomacy" has played an important role in the negotiation process. Specifically, letters, telephone calls and meetings between the leaders of China and the United States have become important ways for the two countries to maintain communication and build consensus on economic and trade issues. The "trilogy" of letters–telephone–meetings has demonstrated its efficiency and effectiveness, particularly at difficult times during the negotiations. Indeed, the leaders' meetings at the G20 Buenos Aires Summit on 1 December 2018 and at the Osaka Summit on 29 June 2019 became important events that helped avoid the immediate escalation of the trade war at critical moments.

Judging from the initiation and evolution of the China–US trade war, the United States is always the active side, which initiated and escalated the trade war, while China is the passive one, which responded by introducing countermeasures. To some extent, this has given the US side a "first mover advantage" during the game in defining its rhythm and direction. In response to the offensive actions from the United States, China has waged relatively restrained countermeasures, despite their nature of tit-for-tat confrontation. It seems that China has somehow followed an equivalent principle. In the first phase of the trade war, it imposed the same tariffs (25%), on the same amount (US$ 50 billion) and at the same rhythm (first US$ 34 billion and then US$ 16 billion) of the US measure, realizing a perfectly equivalent countermeasure. However, this became impossible for the later rounds of the trade war due to the limited "arsenal". In response to the US$ 200 billion tariff measure from the US side during the second round, China imposed tariffs on US$ 60 billion worth of goods with relatively low rates. In the third round, China announced a tariff list of US$ 75 billion in response to the US list of US$ 300 billion. However, a major part of these goods amounting to US$ 75 billion are duplicates of goods in the earlier rounds (Section 3.1).

Before and during the trade war, decision makers need to understand the strengths and weaknesses of themselves vis-à-vis their counterparts, and they need to look both behind and ahead. "Wargames", including scenario exercises and tabletop map exercises, can help them make the right decision without engaging in a real devastating trade warfare. In the complicated game of a trade war, the side in a relatively stronger position is often inclined to "fight", while the weaker side tends to "talk" so as to reach a compromise earlier in order to avoid big harm. However, this is not always the case, as "players" in the game of a trade war often attach less emphasis to future payoffs (Chapter 1, Section 1.3). They may make their decision primarily based on the current scenario and short-term calculation, without a sufficient consideration of subsequent interactions.

Therefore, the timing and timeliness of decisions is crucial. For the weaker side in this regard, early preventive actions are overriding priority, and it is of strategic importance to prevent the trade war from happening. Once the trade warfare starts, it will not be easy to end the fight. In fact, the more escalated the trade war, the more unbalanced the "arsenal" in the trade war would be. In addition, the more stakes that have been put in the game, the more demands and the higher bottom lines can be seen. In the 1980s, Japan had successfully prevented a large-scale trade war with the United States by making necessary concessions at a rather early stage. The country has somehow achieved the goal of "defeating the enemy without fighting". The Japanese understood their dependence on the US market, and they also realized that in trade disputes those with large export scale and huge surplus were the weak side. Overall, it is a rational choice to resolve conflicts through negotiations and avoid intensification of conflicts.

During the trade war, the emergence of a "balance point" is often an opportunity for reconciliation. This point involves the balance of the two sides' abilities both to offend and to defend. The losses suffered by the domestic economy in the trade war are an important consideration, and the constraints of domestic political factors and the influences of interest groups cannot be underestimated.

Notes

1   Gary Clyde Hufbauer and Zhiyao (Lucy) Lu, *The USTR Tariff Exclusion Process: Five Things to Know about These Opaque Handouts*, The Peterson Institute for International Economics, 19 December 2019.
2   "USTR Announces Initiation of Section 301 Investigation of China", *Press Release*, Office of the USTR, 18 August 2017.
3   *Findings of the Investigation into China's Acts, Policies, and Practices Related to Technology Transfer, Intellectual Property, and Innovation under Section 301 of the Trade Act of 1974*, Office of the USTR, 22 March 2018.
4   Presidential Memorandum on the Actions by the United States Related to the Section 301 Investigation, issued on 22 March 2018.
5   The Entity List includes names of selected foreign companies, research institutions, public and private organizations, individuals and other types of legal persons, that are subject to specific license requirements for US companies' exports, reexports and (in-country) transfers of specified items.
6   Alexandra Alper, Toby Sterling, and Stephen Nellis, "Trump Administration Pressed Dutch Hard to Cancel China Chip-Equipment Sale: Sources", *Reuters*, 6 January 2020.
7   *Addressing China's Laws, Policies, Practices, and Actions Related to Intellectual Property, Innovation, and Technology*, US Presidential Memorandum, 14 April 2017.
8   Joint Statement of the United States and China Regarding Trade Consultations, 19 May 2018.
9   "President Donald J. Trump Is Confronting China's Unfair Trade Policies", Fact Sheet, the White House, issued on 29 May 2018.
10   Statement from the Press Secretary Regarding the President's Working Dinner with China, issued on 1 December 2018.
11   "The ninth round of China-US high-level economic and trade consultations has been successfully concluded" (in Chinese), Xinhua News Agency, 6 April 2019.

12 Gary Clyde Hufbauer, "Managed Trade: Centerpiece of China-US Phase One Deal", the Peterson Institute for International Economics, 16 January 2020.
13 The interview of Singapore Prime Minister Lee Hsien Loong with Bloomberg's Editor-in-Chief John Micklethwait at Davos, 23 January 2020.
14 The tariffs imposed by the United States on Chinese exports are as follows: 25% tariff on US$ 250 billion worth of Chinese products and 7.5% tariff on US$ 120 billion worth of Chinese products.
15 The tariffs imposed by China on US exports are as follows: 25% tariff on US$ 50 billion worth of American products; 5%–25% tariff on US$ 60 billion worth of American products and 5%–10% tariff on approximately US$ 10 billion worth of American products.
16 A subgame perfect Nash Equilibrium is an equilibrium such that players' strategies constitute a Nash Equilibrium in every subgame of the original game.

4 The China–US trade war

Impacts and implications

> What benefits the enemy, harms you; and what benefits you, harms the enemy.
>
> – Niccolo Machiavelli

With unprecedented scope and scale, the China–US trade war has become a major factor affecting the Chinese and American economies, as well as an important risk for the world economy. Based on an original analytical framework and existing data up to the end of 2019, this chapter aims to make a comprehensive assessment of economic consequences of this historical trade conflict. It examines relevant economic variables at various levels – macro, meso and micro levels – and from different perspectives – trade and investment diversion, macroeconomic performance and firm behaviour. Due to the diverging economic and trade structures of China and the United States, ramifications of the trade war differ. For China, the impact of "export direction" is primary, as manifested in the reduced exports, industrial output and economic growth. For the United States, by contrast, the impact of "import direction" dominates, reflected in how tariffs affect import prices and consumer welfare, while the "export direction" shock affects a rather limited number of areas, such as agriculture. As the two parties are the world's largest economies and major powers, this chapter also pays attention to some issues with long-term significance, exploring what the trade war means for China–US relations, world economy and the global system as a whole.

4.1 Trade and investment diversion: impacts at the international level

As a cross-border economic phenomenon, trade war affects a country's economy first at the international level. This is mainly reflected in the diversion effect of trade and investment, that is, the shift of trade and investment flows due to special tariffs. The extent of trade and investment diversion depends on many factors – in the case of trade, for instance, the tariff pass-through rate and the prices elasticity of demand (Chapter 1, Section 1.3). By comparing changes before and after the trade war, this section analyzes the extent of diversion effects for international trade, FDI and cross-border portfolio investment, respectively. The coverage of tariffs and the sensitivity of enterprises' decision-making lead to differences among products and industries. The trade war directly affects the specific products on the tariff list and the related industries. However, there have been spillover effects on other products and industries. Therefore, we first look at the aggregate measurement of trade and investment, and then examine the situation of specific products and industries. This is helpful to study the connection between the impact of trade war at international and macro levels.

International trade

The China–US trade war has led to a surge in bilateral tariffs between China and the United States (Chapter 3, Figure 3.2). This has been translated to a considerable degree of trade diversion. The concept "trade diversion" refers to changes in the trade volume of a country triggered by a change in specific policies (trade policies, trade remedies, tariffs, etc.).[1] To be more concrete, under the background of trade war, a specific tariff that Country A imposes on Country B will increase the prices of goods exported from the latter, which will possibly reduce the exports to Country A, and a third party (Country C) will export more to Country A accordingly. In this case, for Country A, part of its imports are diverted from Country B to Country C. As for a specific kind of product, whether trade diversion will happen depends on the real effect of tariffs on prices (the degree of tariff pass-through as discussed in Chapter 1, Section 1.3), the price elasticity of both supply and demand, the existence of import substitution country (Country C) and the comparison in production costs between Country B and Country C. In the short term, Country C needs to expand its product capacities. For specific products, the country may need to build new production facilities in a relatively longer term. Therefore, the capital and time needed for building or expanding productive capacities in an alternative production location is also an influencing factor.

The aggregate trade diversion effect is well reflected by the changes in China and the United States' exports to each other and their proportions in their counterpart's total imports. These data show that both China and the United States have experienced a significant degree of trade diversion since the onset of the trade war. With regard to the timing of these effects, the decline of exports from the United States was earlier, mainly in the second half of 2018, while that for China appeared later, mainly in the first half of 2019. In terms of the specific goods on the tariff lists during the first two phases of the trade war, there has been a downward trend in the export volume of both China and the United States (Cerutti et al., 2019).[2] A similar study finds that US tariffs against China resulted in a reduction in imports of the tariffed Chinese products by more than 25% during the first half of 2019, and China's export losses increased over time (Nicita, 2019).

During the second half of 2018, there was no obvious trade diversion for China at the aggregate level. In fact, total US imports from China went up after the beginning of the trade war, and China accounted for 22% of the United States' overall imports in the second half of 2018, rising from 20% in the first half (Figure 4.1). By contrast, Chinese data show that the import volume from the United States declined right after the onset of the trade war, particularly in the fourth quarter of 2018. Meanwhile, the share of imports from the United States in China's total imports dropped from more than 8% to approximately 6%, indicating a significant trade diversion for the United States due to the trade war. The time lag of the trade diversion for China can be explained by two factors. On the one hand, at the beginning of the trade war, some US importers adopted a wait and see attitude. In other words, they tended to not to change their sourcing patterns as they were not sure how long the tariffs would last. On the other hand, some US importers

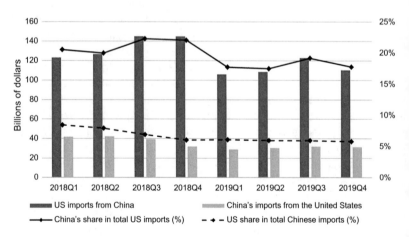

Figure 4.1 Bilateral imports of China and the United States, 2018 and 2019

Source: General Administration of Customs of China; US Census Bureau.

took "pre-emptive actions" by undertaking advance purchases in order to avoid the negative impact of tariffs. Indeed, there was an increase in imports in advance of the effective dates of tariff (Cerutti et al., 2019).

However, the situation has changed since the beginning of 2019: while US exports to China remained stable, the negative impact of the trade war on China's exports to the United States started to unfold (Figure 4.1). Chinese data demonstrate that, in the first quarter of 2019, imports from the United States dropped slightly, but the US share in total Chinese imports remained at 6%. This was partly because China had suspended tariffs on automobiles and auto parts from the United States and agreed to resume soybean imports from the United States. However, the US data show that both the amount of imports from China and its share in total imports of the United States dropped significantly. Imports from China dropped from US$ 145 billion in the last quarter of 2018 to US$ 106 billion in the first quarter of 2019, with China's share declining from 22% to 18%. Monthly data also demonstrate a downward trend: US imports from China in March 2019 dropped to US$ 31 billion, or 15% of the total, surpassed by Mexico for the first time. This took place as US importers started to change their sourcing strategy: as inventories were digested, alternative purchasers were made. In addition, some exporters have started to relocate their production bases away from China.

Statistics from commercial institutions show that containerized cargo shipped from China to the United States declined by 6.4% in the first quarter of 2019, in which some specific kinds of goods are seriously affected. For example, refrigerators imported from China to the United States dropped by 24% in the first quarter, while those imported from Korea and Mexico increased by 32%; tires imported from China dropped by 29% while those imported from Vietnam surged by 142%.[3] Generally, it can be concluded that some Asian countries like Vietnam and some Latin American countries like Mexico whose importing industries are substitutions for those of China are main beneficiary countries of the trade diversion. By comparing US imports of tariffed products during the first two quarters of 2018 and 2019, respectively, an analysis demonstrates that Taiwan Province of China, Mexico, the European Union and Vietnam benefited the most from trade diversion effects of the China–US trade war (Nicita, 2019). With regard to the US$ 50 billion worth of Chinese products as the target of US tariffs during the first phase of the trade war, the share of China in US imports declined from 8.6% in 2018 to 5.5% in the first half of 2019, and Mexico gained most from the trade diversion.

Throughout 2019, exports from China and the United States to each other remain stagnated. In the second quarter, the total imports of China and the United States both increased, but imports between their counterparts remained flat. In the third quarter, both US imports from China and

Chinese imports from the United States increased, but were still lower than the quarterly amount in 2018. In the fourth quarter of 2019, as the performance of US exports to China remined stable, that of China declined. Overall, trade diversion exists for both countries: China's share in total US imports dropped from 21.2% in 2018 to 18.0% in 2019; the US share in total Chinese imports declined from 7.3% to 6.7% during the same period.

As long as the United States keeps importing goods instead of producing domestically, the amount of the US trade deficit will remain the same despite the existence of trade diversion. Therefore, the real impact of the China–US trade war on the US trade deficit depends on whether firms decide to invest and produce locally in the United States. The trade data illustrate a mixed picture. Total deficit in trade in goods of the United States reached US$ 891 billion in 2018, the year when the trade war started, 10.4% more than that in 2017. In 2019, however, the US goods deficit dropped slightly to US$ 866 billion. In the same year, the deficit with China decreased US$ 74 billion to US$ 346 billion.[4] China did suffer from the trade war, but if third party countries take most of China's market share, the overall impact of the trade war on the US trade deficit is rather limited.

Foreign direct investment

In the era of globalization, the increase of international investment and the expansion of global value chains have reshaped the landscape of world trade. The China–US trade war is the first major trade conflict that has taken place against the background of strong globalization (Chapter 1, Section 1.2). Thus, it will not only impact on trade, but will also have strong effects on the patterns of international investment and global production networks. Impact on FDI is manifested in two aspects – both reduced FDI inflows from new investors and shrinking inward FDI stock due to divestments.

Conceptually, FDI flows can suffer from a similar diversion effect like trade flows. MNEs may relocate their production facilities from home to host countries or move their manufacturing and export bases from countries with high tariffs to those with low tariffs, as motivated by "tariff jumping/ hopping" motivations (see e.g. Blonigen, 2002). In the context of a trade war, specific tariffs can affect both supply chain management and international production location of MNEs. A specific tariff that Country A imposes on Country B will raise the price of goods which are produced in Country B and exported to Country A, making Country B less appealing as a manufacturing or export base. Thus, some potential investments will possibly divert from Country B to a third party (Country C), and even some existing production facilities in Country B may be relocated to other countries.

Official FDI data come from the balance of payments (BOP) statistics, covering both cross-border mergers and acquisitions and greenfield investments. To analyze the investment diversion due to trade war, greenfield investment is the main research target. Therefore, we pay attention to the amount of investment of greenfield projects, rather than the total amount of FDI, and examine the quarterly data on greenfield investment in China and the United States during 2018 and the first half of 2019 (Figure 4.2). The ratio between the United States and China's amounts of greenfield investment is used to measure the relative strength of the two countries in attracting international capital.

The picture of greenfield investment also points to a turning point at the beginning of 2019: foreign investment in China was strong in the second half of 2018 but dropped sharply in the first half of 2019 (Figure 4.2). This illustrates that foreign investment was significantly affected by the trade war. As for the United States, the quarterly amount of greenfield investment experienced obvious fluctuations in 2018 with a reduction in the second half of the year. Meanwhile, the number of the US greenfield projects in the second half of the year went up. The investment volume in the United States also dropped considerably in the first half of 2019, especially in the first quarter. It seems that foreign investment in both China and the United States has been negatively affected, owing to the uncertainty arising from the trade war. However, China seems to suffer more, as the quarterly average of foreign greenfield investment declined from US$ 27 billion in 2018

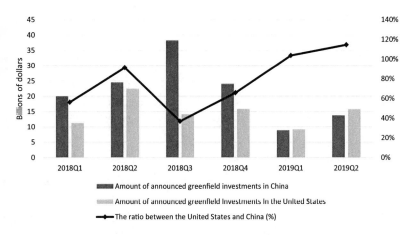

Figure 4.2 Greenfield foreign investment in China and the United States, 2018 and the first half of 2019

Source: fDi Markets.

to US\$ 11 billion in 2019. As a result, the ratio between the United States and China jumped to a level above 100% in the first half of 2019. This demonstrates an increased attractiveness of the United States vis-à-vis China to international investment in the short term.

Data on projects in specific industries show that the increase in greenfield investment in China in the second half of 2018 was primarily driven by manufacturing industries, especially automobiles, chemicals and electronic components. In the industries of highly internationalized production networks, such as electronics, decisions on production location and supply chain configuration are relatively easily affected by the trade war. Nevertheless, what happened in the second half of 2018 did not show such influence, partly due to the time lag of the tariff impact on firms' long-term investment decision. Additionally, major enterprises and large-scale projects played an important role in the steady growth of foreign capital in the second half of 2018, despite the ongoing trade war. Indeed, when the negative effects of tariffs started to unfold, foreign investment in China has been significantly affected since the beginning of 2019.

China's official data show that FDI inflows to the country have remained stable since the outbreak of the trade war. However, there is a significant difference between China's current FDI statistics system and the common international practices, and, as a result, divestment is not reflected in the official numbers. Judging from the specific conditions of various regions and industries, some divestments were the result of the combined effect of higher production costs caused by rising wages and land prices and higher tariffs caused by the trade war. There has been some evidence of divestments in China due specifically to the China–US trade war. For instance, Japanese video game giant Nintendo has shifted production of its Switch console from China to Vietnam; Google has moved its manufacturing business of cloud motherboards and some Nest smart home products to Taiwan Province of China and Malaysia; both HP and Dell plan to relocate most of their PC manufacturing operations to Southeast Asia.[5]

Cross-border portfolio investment

Diversion effects also exist in international portfolio investment, due to investors' changing valuation of specific securities from related countries. Though both FDI and international portfolio investment are in the financial and capital account of the BOP, they show different reactions to the trade war. While the impacts on the FDI have a longer time lag, portfolio investment is more sensitive to the shock from specific events related to the trade war.

After the United States and China announced tariff measures in early April 2018, Chinese stocks experienced two consecutive months of declining net inflows in the global market.[6] Most economies, including China and the United States, experienced significant net outflows in June before the tariffs were formally imposed in July. Since July 2018, capital inflows to Chinese stocks had started to recover in global financial markets. Different from the newly industrialized Asian economies and major emerging economies, Chinese stocks had shown a unique appeal for international capital. In November 2018, capital inflows in Chinese stocks began to decline because of the earlier escalation of the trade war (Chapter 3, Section 3.1). During this period, capital inflows to the Asian and emerging economies began to pick up, while the United States was still dominated by capital outflows.

During the second and third quarters of 2019, foreign investors expressed concerns about further trade war escalations and worries about the deadlock in trade talks between China and the United States. Consequently, more than US$ 13 billion flowed out of Chinese stocks from April to August 2019. At the same time, the escalation of the trade war has negatively affected the stock market performance in many other countries.

4.2 Macroeconomic consequences

Trade war affects the economy at the macro level. Diversion of trade and investment is a major channel through which trade conflicts affect a country's macroeconomic performance, but it is not the only one. In other words, negative effects outside the domain of international economy may also affect the macroeconomy. This embodies, for instance, at the micro level by affecting the decision and behaviour of microeconomic entities (including enterprises, households, etc.), while at the macro level it influences capital formation and final consumption. Therefore, trade wars affect economic growth directly through changes in imports and exports, and indirectly by impacting on investment and consumption.

In terms of the impacts in the "export direction", trade wars can affect GDP growth rate and other economic variables from the following aspects: first, trade diversion decreases export volume, impedes economic growth and affects the BOP; second, investment diversion reduces capital inflows and may also lead to capital outflows due to divestments, thus restricting gross fixed capital formation at the macro level; third, the outbreak and escalation of trade wars affect business confidence, so that enterprises lower their investment expenditures, thus impeding capital formation and economic growth at the macro level; finally, trade wars could harm consumers' confidence and their final expenditures accordingly, therefore affecting economic performance. In all, the first two aspects, trade and investment diversion effects (Section 4.1) manifest at the international level and are relatively direct, while the latter two aspects reflect impacts on domestic enterprises and consumers and are somehow indirect.

China's economic growth is considerably affected by the trade war. The latest updated data demonstrate that China's quarterly GDP growth rate fluctuated within a very narrow range between 6.8% to 7.0% since the beginning of 2016, and then started to decline since mid-2018 (Figure 4.3). Official data show that, in the third and fourth quarters of 2019, this figure went to 6.0% – the lowest level since the early 1990s. For China, the growth rate of 6% is a threshold level. On the one hand, the target of the annual growth rate for 2019 has been set within the range 6.0–6.5%. On the other hand, to achieve the growth target of the 13th Five-Year Plan and the long-term objective of four-fold growth up to 2020, an annual GDP growth rate above 6% is needed for both 2019 and 2020. Employment is another concern, as many jobs will be lost if exports continue to drop.

On the United States' side, employment remains strong, but economic growth has slowed down (Figure 4.3). Compared with China, quarterly economic growth in the United States experiences remarkable fluctuation. US economic growth has an upward trend from the first quarter of 2016 until the third first quarter of 2018 but plunged in the last quarter of the year. In 2019, the economy remained stable, but some signals of an economic recession had appeared. Looking into the future, the implementation of the Phase One agreement is likely to give a strong boost to the growth of the US economy.

Trade is not the major reason for China's sluggish economic growth. The situation in the second half of 2018 illustrates that the decline in China's economic growth was not caused by trade diversion (Section 4.1). Indeed, China's total surplus in trade in goods amounted to US$ 352 billion in 2018, a decline by 16.2% year-on-year, indicating that net exports did affect GDP growth. However, it was not the trade war that led to this decline. In fact, China's goods surplus with the United States was US$ 323 billion, increased by 17.2%. Therefore, China's trade with the United States continues to be the main source of China's trade surplus and is still one of the key factors promoting economic growth.

The main problem for China is the dwindling business confidence. The contribution of net exports of commodities and services to China's GDP growth was negative during the first three quarters of 2018. It turned positive in the fourth quarter. In the first quarter of 2019, the contribution of net exports to GDP growth surged to 19%, which was rare in recent years. One key reason for that is the trade surplus with the United States. Custom data show that, in the first quarter, China's exports to the United States dropped slightly

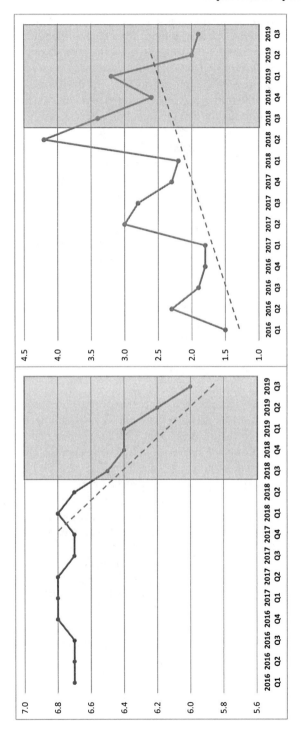

Figure 4.3 Quarterly GDP growth rates of China and the United States, 2016–2019

Source: National Bureau of Statistics of China; US Bureau of Economic Analysis.

by 3.7% to US$ 92 billion, whilst imports from the United States declined significantly by 28.3% to US$ 28 billion, which led to the sharp increase in China's trade surplus with the United States. However, the contribution of gross fixed capital formation to GDP growth decreased from around 40% in the first three quarters of 2018 to 18% in the first quarter of 2019. This shows that Chinese enterprises had less incentives to invest, which seems to be a major channel through which the trade war affects China's economic growth. Capital formation's contribution to GDP growth remained at a relatively low level then and started to surge in the last quarter of 2019 as a result of strengthened policy efforts to boost the economy.

In the imbalanced bilateral trade pattern, the United States is mainly an importer (Chapter 2, Section 2.2). On the second tariff list that the United States announced (the US$ 200 billion tariff list), more than one-fifth of the consumer goods are closely related to people's daily life.[7] Different from China, the United States' major concern about the impact of the trade war is from the "import direction". This is mainly reflected by the effects on the US consumers and commodity prices due to the US tariffs on Chinese imports. Studies show that because of a large increase in prices of both intermediate products and final products in 2018, nearly all of the tariffs that the United States imposed on other countries have transferred to the prices of imported products, and the US consumers are those who bear the corresponding losses (Amiti et al., 2019a; Fajgelbaum et al., 2019). According to these studies, similar effects also exist in other countries that impose retaliatory tariffs on the United States.

The degree of specific tariffs and the extent of price increase affect the distribution of welfare loss between the exporter and the importer, while the difference between the import and the retail prices determines the distribution of the impact of price increases between the importer and the consumers. Empirical studies show that, after imposing tariffs on China, the increase in import prices was roughly equal to the amount of the tariffs, which means that the United States, especially US customers, had taken all the losses due to tariffs.[8] It is estimated that the first two rounds of specific tariffs the United States imposed on China (US$ 50 billion of 25% and US$ 200 billion of 10%) have brought an annual cost of US$ 420 to each US family, two-thirds of which come from extra expenditures and the rest come from performance loss. Increasing the tariffs for US$ 200 billion imports from 10% to 25% would generate an annual cost of US$ 830 to each US household (Amiti et al., 2019b).

The impact of the China–US trade war on the real economy is primary, but the financial effects cannot be overlooked. They are mainly reflected in the trade war's influences on stock markets and exchange rates. The stock market is not only a "barometer" of the economy, but also a measure and amplifier of economic impacts of the trade confrontation and associated negotiation. In fact, enterprises and individuals can somehow assess the market reaction to the trade war by observing stock prices. In addition, the performance of major stock indexes may affect the negotiators' judgement about impacts of the trade war on their respective economies, and therefore influence the position and process of the trade negotiations. In general, the trade war affects stock markets in both China and the United States, but it has shocked the former much more than the latter. Nine months after 22 March 2018, when the Presidential Memorandum that authorized Section 301 tariff actions against China was released, the S&P 500 of the United States dropped 11%, while the CSI of China plumped by 26% (Figure 4.4). By the end of 2019, the former index had increased to a level 22% higher than that on 22 March 2018, while the increase of the latter index was only 2%.

After a period of clearly diverging trends between March and September 2019, the S&P 500 and the CSI demonstrated a certain degree of correlation during their ups and downs, which were closely related to the China–US trade war and trade talks. From the perspective of the United States, an important reason for its willingness to speed up negotiations with China in December 2018 was that both the US economy and its stock market were weak in the last quarter of the year partly because of the influences of the ongoing trade war with China. However, throughout 2019, the American

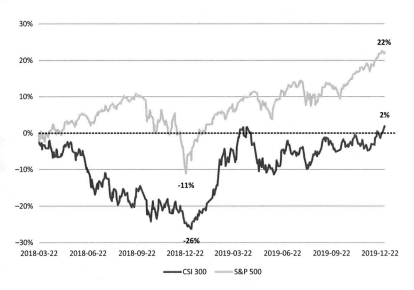

Figure 4.4 Stock market indexes in China and the United States: March 2018–December 2019

economy and stock market performed very well, giving the US side a very strong bargaining power in its trade negotiations with China. The most significant rise of the Chinese stock market was between late-December 2018 and mid- and late-April 2019 (Figure 4.4), when several rounds of intensive and constructive talks were held with the United States (Chapter 3, Section 3.2). Unfortunately, it was interrupted by a major setback in negotiations in early May and the subsequent escalation of the trade war (Chapter 3, Section 3.1).

The fiscal impacts of the trade war reflect mainly the positive effect caused by a rise in the government's tariff revenue and the negative effect due to the subsidies paid to major producers who suffer from the imposed tariffs. As for the United States, the government revenue generated from increased tariffs reached US$ 19 billion from July 2018 to May 2019; however, the subsidies paid to farmers who suffered losses due to the China–US trade war were as high as US$ 25 billion. In conclusion, the net fiscal effect in the early stage of the trade war is negative.[9]

The Chinese economy will continue to suffer from impacts of the "export direction", with exports, firms' investment and economic growth negatively affected. In addition, the implementation of the Phase One agreement will add pressures on China's economic growth. As the US tariffs remain, the American economy will continue to experience their negative effects from the "import direction", as prices increase, and consumer welfare suffers. Thus, it is in the common interest of China and the United States to seek a quick end to the trade war.

4.3 Firm-level effects

Trade wars affect a country's economy mostly through impacting on microeconomic entities. At the "export direction", the direct impact of a trade war on enterprises is mainly reflected on how special tariffs affect the competitiveness of exporting firms. Since the responsible entity for paying import duties is the consignee of imported goods, specific tariffs are actually paid by the importers. Therefore, the consequence of tariffs on specific exporters depends on what actions importers will take when facing a specific tariff, which is also related to the "export direction" impacts of the tariffs (Section 4.2).

Importers have several choices when they are obliged to pay specific tariffs: 1) they can import from other countries instead of the existing one to avoid tariffs; 2) they can pay the tariffs but ask exporters for a price cut so as to shift part of, or even all of, the tariffs to the exporters; 3) they can pay the tariffs while raising prices and thus shift the tariff costs to consumers; or 4) they can swallow the tariffs by themselves without changing prices. At the aggregate level, this will affect the tariff pass-through rate

(Chapter 1, Section 1.3). Under the situation where there are no ideal import substitution countries, importers may choose one from options 2, 3 and 4 or a combination of options 2 and 3. For exporters, the first choice means that they will lose their market, while the second one means that they have to sacrifice part of their profits. If importers raise the prices but not as much as the tariffs, importers and consumers will share the costs. Studies on the China–US trade war show that the tariff costs have been mainly passed to US customers, and the rest are borne by US importers (Cavallo et al., 2019).

Impacts of trade wars on enterprises' decisions and behaviour involve several aspects of the international economy, including trade, investment, offshoring and contract manufacturing, etc. There are two questions that are of vital importance. The first is how much the supply chains of importers are shifted and diversified, and the second is to what extent the producers' decision on production location is affected. Influences vary significantly among industries, companies and products, and they add up to determine the impacts of the trade war at the macro level. To be more specific, the shift and diversification of importers' supply chains determine the degree of trade diversion, while the decision on production location of existing and potential producers/exporters affects the degree of investment diversion (Section 4.1). A questionnaire on more than 200 American MNEs that operate business in China shows that 60% of them will adjust their strategies due to the trade war, 50% will seek new procurement partners and 25% will shift their investment to other countries.[10]

Trade wars affect companies' decisions and behaviour in a complicated manner, which is related to industry characteristics (such as international competition situation), product classification (consumer goods or intermediate products), the overall pattern of value chains, the relationship and relative strength between companies along the value chain, and the scale and duration of tariffs. The supply chains of importers are more difficult to transfer when producers have high cost advantages, higher brand loyalty and more stable upstream and downstream relationships. Time dimension deserves particular attention. At the beginning of the trade war, many importers wait and see, and they tend to raise prices or cut profits in order to deal with uncertainty. As time goes by, however, they reinforce the diversification of the supply chains that may involve every part of enterprise operation. This to some degree offers an interpretation for why trade diversion for China was not that obvious in the early stage but intensified later (Section 4.1). During a specific period, trade diversion tends to self-reinforce and mutually promote with investment diversion. If the influence of trade war on enterprise decision-making changes from short-term to long-term and from reversible to irreversible, its distortion effect on supply chain, investment and production location will intensify.

The trade war distorts global value chains by affecting decisions and behaviour of enterprises, thus affecting the economic and geographical layout of related industries. Generally, due to the China–US trade war, the concentration of sourcing, investment and production in China will decrease, which is associated with the decision of US enterprises, possibly with MNEs from other countries, and even with Chinese enterprises. However, the adjustment in the short run is at the cost of wasting economic resources and reducing economic performance. In the long run, whether the adjustment is beneficial depends on the comparison between the new and old patterns of international production.

For firms, the rise of tariffs and trade barriers is troubling, but increased policy uncertainty can also be costly (Handley and Limão, 2019). In the case of China, the trade war affects particularly foreign companies operating in China and Chinese companies exporting to the United States. However, it also affects Chinese enterprises at large. For the Chinese economy, there is a paradox of impacts of the trade war at the international level (Section 4.1) and at the macro level (Section 4.2) in the second half of 2018. At the aggregate level, the export performance of China was not affected, but the macroeconomic influences were significant. The reason for this paradox lies in the general negative effects of the trade war at the enterprise level. Generally speaking, the short-term negative impact of trade war on China's economy is mainly realized by increasing policy uncertainty, attacking the confidence of Chinese enterprises and further weakening their capital expenditure.

An empirical study examines the impact of tariffs on firms' stock market performance, demonstrating that firms' stock price responses are determined by the degree of their direct exposure to the China–US trade and their indirect exposure through the global value chains (Huang et al., 2019). Similarly, using the event study method (see e.g. Greenland et al., 2018) and a sample of listed companies, our quantitative analysis shows that the overall anticipation of the Chinese stock market to the trade war is negative.

4.4 Broader implications

The China–US trade war has reshaped the bilateral economic relationship between the two countries: extremely high tariffs have become the new normal, firms' sourcing and investment decisions have been largely distorted, and economic exchanges in general have been weakened. At the global level, the trade war has become a major risk for the world economy, dragging down growth forecasts. Its long-term economic, strategic and geopolitical implications cannot be underestimated for the China–US relations and the global economic governance. Is the China–US trade war a first step towards the "Thucydides Trap", however? The answer is no, but the danger for an "economic cold war" is real.

Bilateral economic relationship: will decoupling happen?

After the outbreak of the China–US trade war in 2018, bilateral tariffs surged (Chapter 3). Normal trade flows have been significantly affected by this new normal of high tariffs (Section 4.1). By affecting firms' decisions on sourcing and investing abroad (Section 4.3), the trade war affects both trade and investment patterns, and therefore the degree to which the Chinese and American economies depend on each other. In case trade diversion takes place, the US imports will shift from China to other countries. Its overall trade deficit remains, but the United States reduces its dependence on China. This implies the "decoupling" between American and Chinese economies from the trade perspective, which has been happening. A similar process occurs in other areas, including mutual FDI, technology transfer and other forms of economic exchanges.

The question is, to what extent will the "decoupling" process reach? If a significant degree of decoupling is realized, what will be the costs and implications for the two countries? For China, decoupling is not an option: diversification seems to be a way out, but there is no economy in the world that can replace the role of the United States. For the United States, competitiveness and prosperity will not end, but will be greatly reduced. Apparently, the "decoupling" with China will not be able to help make the United States great again. Overall, a restructuring rather than the decoupling of the economic ties between the United States and China is the rational choice for both sides. China needs a new development model. This model is not one without intensive economic exchanges with the United States, but one which is more compatible with the economic systems of other countries, particularly the United States.

The demand of structural changes from the US side has significant implications for China's existing economic system and development model. Since December 2018, the two countries have agreed in principle on the overall direction of these changes. Even during the trade negotiations, China has introduced considerable policy changes partly in response to the US demand, including for instance, the downplay of the Made in China 2025 initiative and the promulgation of the new Foreign Investment Law. The Phase One agreement will help reduce trade deficit or induce structural changes of the Chinese economy. The future agreement(s), if any, will do more.

World economy: China–US trade war poses a major risk

The trade war has caused losses to both China and the United States. There are also third parties who have suffered or benefited from the war. For the latter, the benefits include two aspects. First, the "substantive gains" refer to export substitution in the relatively short term and production relocation in the relatively long term. Among the major large emerging economies: India generally emphasizes the alternative export opportunities to the United States brought about by the China–US trade war; Brazil focuses on alternative export opportunities to China in areas such as soybeans; and Russia can also benefit as a substitute exporter. From a regional perspective, some countries, such as Japan and South Korea, may suffer from a decrease in their exports of intermediate products to China, and other countries, such as Vietnam and Malaysia, will benefit from replacing China's exports to the United States or the relocation of production bases from China. Second, the "strategic gains" refer to the (perhaps temporarily) eased economic and trade frictions with the United States due to its focus on the trade war between China. For example, both Japan and Germany have very large trade surpluses with the United States and are therefore under great pressure. However, as the United States is targeting China, the friction with Japan and the European Union (including Germany) has been eased.

From a global perspective, the China–US trade war has become a risk for the global economy due to its negative impacts on the world's two largest economies and some third party economies, as well as a wide range of direct and indirect ramifications, including market turmoil, reduced investment and lower productivity due to supply chain disruptions. Several international organizations, such as the IMF and the OECD, consider the unresolved trade war between the United States and China as the biggest known risk to worldwide economic growth and have undertaken downward regions in their estimates in 2019. The IMF estimates that, by 2020, tariffs would translate into a loss of US$ 700 billion, or 0.8% of global GDP. Accordingly, its projected 2019 growth is down from 3.2% to 3.0%, the lowest level since the 2008 global crisis. According to IMF, this is due to a sharp deterioration in manufacturing activity and global trade, with higher tariffs and prolonged trade policy uncertainty damaging investment and demand for capital goods.[11]

The China–US trade war also poses a serious threat to the rule-based multilateral trading system. The global trading system has been undergoing fundamental changes. This is driven by three major forces: 1) efforts to reform the WTO by its key developed members; 2) (re)negotiations of several major regional and bilateral trade agreements led by the United States; and 3) the unprecedented trade war between the United States and China. The two involved countries are the two largest trading nations and among the most influential members of the WTO. Their economic and trade tensions are detrimental to the functioning of the multilateral trading system and the revival of the WTO. During the trade war, indeed, the WTO has become a battlefield of the two countries, involving heated debates on issues such as developing country status and the associated special and differentiated treatment. The dispute settlement mechanism of the WTO has become dysfunctional, as new appointments of the Appellate Body have been blocked by the United States. Furthermore, the Phase One agreement between the two countries may also post a threat to the non-discrimination principle of MFN at the WTO (Chapter 3, Section 3.2).

Long-term China–US relation: "Thucydides Trap" and the global order

The outbreak of the China–US trade war marked a pivotal moment in the long-term relations between China and the United States. Economic mutual dependence between the two counties has been weakened, and strategic trust harmed. In addition, the trade war has somehow altered the strategic positioning of the two countries in the global power landscape: China changes from a more offensive position to a more defensive one, while the United States does the opposite.

Due partly to the China–US trade war, uncertainty in the existing global order has increased. The trade war has significant implications for the multilateral trading regime and the global economic governance at large. Without a quick ending, it will harm multilateralism. Furthermore, there appears a probability of a "great fracture": "the world splitting in two, with the two largest economies on earth creating two separate and competing worlds, each with their own dominant currency, trade and financial rules, their own internet and artificial intelligence capacities, and their own zero sum geopolitical and military strategies".[12] With the trade war as a milestone, the China–US relationship has entered a new era. Can the two countries avoid the "Thucydides Trap", the hypothesis of which states that "when one great power threatens to displace another, war is almost always the result"?[13] For the two nuclear powers, a "hot war" is highly unlikely, neither does a full-scale "new cold war" bear a high chance. However, the danger of China and the United States sliding into an "economic cold war" is real.

The China–US trade war hits globalization and accelerates de-globalization. The rising tariffs have largely weakened institutional support to globalization, though they are mainly between the world's largest two economies. In addition, the reduced and distorted trade and investment flows and the decoupling between China and the United States highlight an accelerated process of de-globalization, which has been gaining ground over the past few years (Chapter 2, Section 2.1).

The China–US trade war also opens a Pandora's Box. In the area of international economic exchange, the failure of the rule-based multilateral system and the prevalence of power-based unilateral actions mean that "la loi de la jungle" apply in international economic relations. President Trump has proudly called himself a "Tariff Man",[14] and the United States has imposed or threatened to impose tariffs to put pressure on other countries for various reasons – including its trade and technology dispute with China, its migration problem with Mexico and its disagreement with France about the digital tax. With these "successful" precedents, spillovers may occur, as economic means become increasingly important in international politics, geopolitical tensions and diplomacy, with trade wars becoming a long-lasting threat for the world.

Notes

1 The concept of trade creation and diversion was first brought up by Jacob Viner (1950), being used to analyze the impact of economic integration on trade patterns.
2 Data resources: the US Department of Commerce; calculated by IMF staff.
3 Data resource: Panjiva Inc.
4 Data resources: the US Census Bureau and the US Bureau of Economic Analysis.
5 Takashi Mochizuki, "Nintendo Moves Some Switch Production Out of China, Adapting to Tariff Threat", *The Wall Street Journal*, 12 June 2019; Justin Scheck, "Dell Plans to Sell Factories in Effort to Cut Costs", *The Wall Street Journal*, 5 September 2018; Debby Wu and Mark Bergen, "Google Is Moving More Hardware Production Out of China", *Bloomberg*, 11 June 2019.
6 Net inflows refer to new investments of current sample funds on a country's securities (Source: EPFR Global).
7 Hongyan Zhao and Liugang Sheng, "Quantitative Analysis of the Impacts of the $200 Billion Tariff List of US", *FTChinese.com*, 1 August 2018.
8 Data of US import prices are from the US Bureau of Labor Statistics.
9 Tariff data are from the US Customs and Border Protection (CBP); data on farmers' subsidies are from the US Department of Agriculture and have been added up.
10 Source: Bain & Company.
11 Transcript of October 2019 World Economic Outlook Press Briefing, IMF, 15 October 2019.
12 UN Secretary-General António Guterres' remarks at the opening of the 74th session of the General Assembly in New York on 24 September 2019.
13 Graham Allison coined this concept in his book *Destined For War: Can America and China escape Thucydides's Trap*, published in 2017.
14 "I am a Tariff Man. When people or countries come in to raid the great wealth of our Nation, I want them to pay for the privilege of doing so. It will always be the best way to max out our economic power …", President Trump's Twitter post on 4 December 2018.

Conclusion

In the summer of 2018, China and the United States slid into a trade war, which has since escalated and become a major risk affecting the economies of both countries as well as the world. The scale of the trade war is unprecedented, as a major part of their mutual exports has been put under the "fire" of special tariffs. As far as China is concerned, exports affected by the tariff had reached about US\$ 360 billion by September 2019. For the US side, affected exports could be estimated at around US\$ 120 billion. Obviously, due to the imbalance in China–US trade, the "arsenal" for fighting a trade war is highly unbalanced.

There are some common features between this trade war and its precedents in the world economic history, but the China–US trade war has become unique in many senses. First, a whole economy, rather than specific sectors, is targeted against a backdrop of some fundamental changes happening at the national and global levels (Chapter 2). Second, different from the traditional pattern of "threat-concession" in the past, the China–US trade war demonstrates a new tit-for-tat model – an iteration of games of "tariff measures-countermeasure" (Chapter 3). Third, conflicts in the fields of trade and technology are intertwined, and there have been signs of escalation to other areas and the emergence of an extreme demand of "decoupling". Fourth, the scale of the trade war, in terms of the affected trade flows and tariff rates, the scope and intensity of various policy measures, and their impacts and implications are unprecedented, demonstrating a fierce confrontation between the world's two major (economic) powers (Chapters 3 and 4).

The ramifications of the trade war on the American and Chinese economies differ, because of the size and structure of their trade and economies. For the former, it is mainly from the "import direction", as reflected in the rising price of imported goods and reduced consumer welfare. For the latter, it is primarily from the "export direction", first internationally on exports and FDI inflows, and then domestically on industrial production, employment and economic growth. At the micro level, both exporters and enterprises in general have been negatively affected in China, and the eroding business confidence has become a major factor influencing the scale of capital formation and the speed of economic growth (Chapter 4). As the first major trade conflict against the background of strong globalization, the China–US trade war has had significant effects on the patterns of international investment and global value chains. Here the time dimension matters. As the trade war continues and escalates, the early wait-and-see attitude of enterprises has changed, with their decisions on procurement and investment strongly affected. If the influence changes from short- to long-term and from reversible to irreversible, its distortion effect on supply chain, investment and production location will intensify.

The China–US trade war involves a very complicated process of "fighting while talking". By October 2019, the two sides had engaged in three principal phases of "tariff combat" and undertaken 13 rounds of major trade negotiations. In this process, trade, science and technology, finance (exchange rates) and investment issues are intertwined, economic and political considerations are intertwined, and international and domestic politics are intertwined. With the gradual escalation of the trade conflict, the stakes have increased, and the demands and bottom lines of both sides are also evolving. Finally, the 13th round of trade talks held in October 2019 made a breakthrough and the two sides agreed on the Phase One agreement, which was signed later in January 2020. It seems that, facing enormous challenges, the negotiators decided to sort out all aspects of problems and tried to agree on some easier ones. As the result of this early harvest approach, the Phase One agreement prevented the implementation of a new round of tariffs planed for December 2019, though it only marginally rolled back the existing tariffs. Overall, it has become a turning point of the trade war and a key step for its de-escalation.

It remains uncertain when the historical trade war will finally end. By February 2020, China had removed a major part of its tariffs in order to fulfil its commitments in the Phase One agreement for increasing US imports by US$ 200 billion in two years. By contrast, the United States maintains its 25% tariffs on US$ 250 billion worth of Chinese imports, with 7.5% tariffs on another US$ 120 billion. Therefore, the effects of tariffs will continue to unfold. In terms of the macroeconomic impact, the implementation of the Phase One agreement will assert an additional influence. For the Chinese economy the downward pressure from this agreement will be added to the existing effect of tariffs, while for the United States the implementation of the agreement will provide a strong stimulating effect to its economic growth. This imbalance, together with the unexpected shock from the COVID-19 pandemic, will affect the stances of the two countries during follow-up negotiations and therefore the final outcomes of the trade war. There is no denying that the negotiators still face great challenges.

The China–US trade war is undoubtedly a major trade and economic clash between the world's first and second largest economies. This unprecedented clash has been taking place between an incumbent superpower and an emerging "superpower" of great cultural and ideological differences. Without effective control, therefore, the trade war may become the precursor of an "economic cold war", a full-fledged strategic confrontation, and a "great fracture" that splits the world in two. Because of this, the importance of the ongoing trade negotiations between China and the United States cannot be overemphasized, and its complexity and difficulty cannot be overestimated.

Looking into the future, there are several questions worth considering about the final result of the China–US trade war, the upcoming path of the economic and trade relationship between China and the United States, and the uncertain future of the bilateral relation between the world's two major powers:

- *Two possibilities of the trade war.* China and the United States had realized a "ceasefire" by reaching the Phase One trade agreement. As three rounds of "tariff combat" took place, perhaps one or two more phases of negotiations and trade agreements are needed to bring tariffs back to normal. In the upcoming phases of negotiation, there will be two possibilities. First, both sides choose to take a step back and try to reach agreements to end the trade war within a relatively short period of time. Second, the two sides stand deadlocked and the trade war continues, and only when serious negative impacts emerge and/or fundamental political changes occur can the two sides make major compromises.
- *Two paths of the bilateral economic relationship.* There may be two completely different paths in the evolution of China–US economic and trade relations. First, taking a possible breakthrough in trade talks as an opportunity for the sufficient coordination of economic systems, the bilateral economic relationship remains basically stable. Second, trade war lasts long, economic systems cannot be reconciled, and American and Chinese economies gradually decouple.
- *Two futures of China–US relations.* From a broader perspective, there are also two possibilities for the future evolution of China–US bilateral relations. First, China and the United States maintain their "economic synergy" through system adjustment and harmonization, which will help safeguard a basic stability in China–US relations and hopefully the realization of common prosperity in both countries. Second, the

positive role of economy and trade in the relations between the two countries is weakened and the negative effect is enhanced, thus causing the bilateral relations to continue to be tense and deteriorating.

These two possibilities, two paths and two futures are closely related. Breakthroughs in the upcoming phases of trade negotiations are expected to lead to a path of sound evolution of economic and broader relationship between China and the United States and shape the future of common prosperity between the two countries. On the contrary, if the negotiations are deadlocked, the trade war may turn again into a seesaw battle, and its negative impact on the economies of both sides will continue to be released. If negotiations break down, the trade confrontation further escalates and technological as well as financial conflicts intensify, the "economic cold war" between the world's two major powers will begin. The risk of this geo-economic battle for the world economy cannot be underestimated, and the COVID-19 pandemic has added the danger.

The current troubles facing China and the United States stem from the dissatisfaction and uneasiness of the United States about the status quo, as well as its intentions and actions to try to change it. The use of such unconventional means as a trade war cannot be separated from the "soil" of domestic politics in the United States and the "climate" of the evolution of China–US bilateral relations. Extreme measures and maximum pressure are challenging China's interests and dignity and America's own interests and values. However, the initiation and escalation of the trade war mean that the old equilibrium between China and the United States has been broken. Accordingly, they need to find a new balance based on realistic judgement and rational thinking.

First, find a new balance for the next phase of trade agreements in order to end the trade war in a relatively short period of time. China and the United States need to maintain the momentum of negotiations and seek a balance of interests through effective negotiations and necessary concessions. After the "early harvest" of the Phase One agreement, however, negotiators face more differences and difficulties. In particular, a number of remaining structural changes, such as those related to SOEs and industrial subsidies, are central to China's basic development model. In addition, China has already offered a US$ 200 billion purchase package in the Phase One agreement. Therefore, the room for further compromise has narrowed, with bargaining chips reduced. By contrast, the United States maintains its maximum pressure on China by keeping the tariffs. All these make it difficult to find the balance point for a new trade deal.

Second, in the medium term, find a new balance in the economic and trade relations between the two countries. Quantified purchase is an old method for addressing trade imbalances. It has limitations and problems, such as distorting markets, breaking rules and hurting third parties. Therefore, China and the United States need to think about institutional arrangements to promote bilateral trade flows and reduce imbalances, and the principles of zero tariffs, zero non-tariff barriers and zero subsidies can be discussed in the future. In terms of investment, there is much room for both sides to increase market access to each other. In the meantime, it is advisable to encourage Chinese enterprises to implement large-scale greenfield investment projects and create jobs in the United States. Negotiations of the bilateral investment treat between China and the United States has been suspended since end-2016. If a breakthrough could be made in this area, it would lay the institutional foundation for promoting two-way investment between the two countries.

Third, in the long run, find a new balance between the two countries' economic systems. Some regard the China–US trade war as a prelude to the struggle for world hegemony in the 21st century. Facing doubts based on the thinking of geopolitical conflicts and civilization clashes, China will adhere to its path and philosophy of "peaceful rise". From an economic point of view, the country will further improve its economic system and development model. What is important is that China needs to improve the "compatibility" of its economic system and development model with the rest of the world. This will help establish a sound international position corresponding to its economic scale and contribution. There are many specific issues, but the foremost is to find a new balance between the economic systems of China and the United States. At the level of implementation, the adoption of a policy principle of competition neutrality and its application in the areas of industrial policy and SOE regime would be helpful.

China and the United States are still in the painful process of finding a "new equilibrium" between their economies. The United States emphasizes a fair and reciprocal economic relation, while China needs a stable and predictable trade arrangement conducive to its long-term economic development. Such an arrangement requires both open external markets and fair international rules. From a conceptual viewpoint, the "fairness" demanded by the United States and the "predictability" demanded by China are not irreconcilable. In addition, market economy and free trade are both recognized by the two countries. Although there are huge differences, therefore, it is still possible for the two sides to find the necessary intersection to reach a grand consensus.

In the face of the crossroads in China–US relations, political leaders in both countries should be cautious to prevent the two countries from sliding into a "full-fledged confrontation". Both sides need to make adjustments in order to accommodate each other. In terms of the positioning of bilateral relations, China and the United States have long been speaking their own language. In particular, the United States has started to define China as a "strategic competitor", while China has always been advocating a so-called "new type of power relationship". Is there a middle ground on which strategic mutual trust can be established? In fact, cooperation and competition coexist between the two countries, and cooperation plays a fundamental role. Therefore, we believe that a "constructive coopetition based on cooperation" is a rather rational orientation for China–US relations, while "a global partnership for peace and development" could be a long-term goal.

Competition between China and the Unites States exists objectively, but it needs to be based on carefully designed, reasonable and enforceable rules. These rules are ideally at the multilateral level, but bilateral arrangements are the realistic solution. These rules need to set strict constraints for the bilateral competition, so that they do not challenge each other's core interests. Controlling differences and avoiding conflicts are the bottom line, and the ongoing trade war is a severe test for both countries.

Appendices

Appendix 1

A brief chronology of the China–US trade war: tariff measures and trade negotiations

Date	Trade war (tariff measures)	Trade negotiation
2018/02/27–03/03		Round 1 of Economic and Trade Consultations, Washington
03/22	US president signed a memorandum to authorize tariffs and other measures	
04/03	USTR announces US$ 50 billion tariff list	
04/04	China announces US$ 50 billion tariff list	
05/03–04		Round 2 of Economic and Trade Consultations, Beijing
05/15–19		Round 3 of Economic and Trade Consultations, Washington
06/02–04		Round 4 of Economic and Trade Consultations, Beijing
06/15	USTR announces US$ 50 billion tariff list (final)	
06/16	China announces US$ 50 billion tariff list (final)	
07/06	First part of the first phase US$ 34 billion, 25% tariffs come into effect	
07/10	USTR announces US$ 200 billion tariff list	
08/03	China announces US$ 60 billion tariff list	
08/22–23		A major vice ministerial-level consultation, Washington

Date	Trade war (tariff measures)	Trade negotiation
08/23	Second part of the first phase US$ 16 billion, 25% tariffs come into effect	
09/17	USTR announces US$ 200 billion tariff list (final)	
09/18	China announces implementation of a US$ 60 billion tariff list	
09/24	Second phase US$ 200 billion (10%) and US$ 60 billion (5 and 10%) tariffs take effect	
11/01		Chinese and American leaders speak by phone
12/01		China–US Heads of State meeting at G20 Summit in Argentina
2019/01/07–08		A major vice ministerial-level consultation, Beijing
01/30–31		Round 5 of Economic and Trade Consultations, Washington
02/14–15		Round 6 of Economic and Trade Consultations, Beijing
02/21–24		Round 7 of Economic and Trade Consultations, Washington
03/28–29		Round 8 of Economic and Trade Consultations, Beijing
04/03–05		Round 9 of Economic and Trade Consultations, Washington
04/30–05/01		Round 10 of Economic and Trade Consultations, Beijing
05/09	USTR announces US$ 200 billion tariff upgrade	
05/09–10		Round 11 of Economic and Trade Consultations, Washington
05/13	China announces US$ 60 billion tariff upgrade	
06/01(15)	Second phase tariffs upgrade: US$ 200 billion (25%) and US$ 60 billion (5, 10, 20, 25%)	

Date	Trade war (tariff measures)	Trade negotiation
06/18		Chinese and American leaders speak by phone
06/29		China–US Heads of State meeting at G20 Summit in Japan
07/30–31		Round 12 of Economic and Trade Consultations, Shanghai
08/01	US president announces 10% tariffs on US$ 300 billion	
08/13	USTR announces US$ 300 billion tariff implementation plan	
08/23	China announces US$ 75 billion additional tariff list	
08/23	US president announced an additional 5% tariff on all Chinese goods	
09/01	Third phase (first part) US$ 112 billion (15%) and part of US$ 75 billion tariffs take effect	
		A major vice ministerial-level consultation, Washington
10/09–10		Round 13 of Economic and Trade Consultations, Washington
12/13		China and the US announce the reach of the Phase One trade agreement
12/15	Third phase (second part) US$ 165 billion and another part of $75 billion tariffs postpone	
2020/01/15		Signing of the Phase One trade agreement in Washington
02/14	Third phase (first part) tariffs halve	Phase One trade agreement takes effect

Notes:
1. Major phases of the trade war are shaded.
2. Economic and Trade Consultations = China–US High-level Economic and Trade Consultations.

Appendix 2

A brief chronology of the China–US trade war: technology- and finance-related measures

Date	Sanction and related event
2018/04/16	US Commerce Department announces seven-year ban on ZTE
05/25	Leaders of the two countries speak by phone on ZTE
06/05	ZTE reaches initial agreement with the US government
07/13	US Department of Commerce announces lifting ban on ZTE
12/01	Meng Wanzhou, CFO of Huawei, arrested in Canada
12	US Department of Defence presses the Dutch government for ASML sales of EUV machine
2019/01/28	US Justice Department accuses Huawei and Meng Wanzhou
03/06	Huawei sues the US government on the unfair product ban
05/16	US president signs executive decree on foreign telecommunication equipment
05/17	US Department of Commerce lists Huawei and its affiliated companies on the entity list
05/31	China announces the establishment of "unreliable entity list" system
06/21	US Commerce Department adds five Chinese technology companies to the entity list
06/25	US judges say that three Chinese Banks refuse to obey summons
06/29	China–US Heads of State meeting at G20 Japan Summit, discussing Huawei
08/05	US Treasury identifies China as "currency manipulator"
10/08	US Commerce Department adds eight technology Chinese companies to the entity list
2020/01/03	US Commerce Department takes measures to restrict exports of artificial intelligence software
01/13	US Treasury removes China's designation as a currency manipulator
02/12	The US government accuses Huawei of spying by exploiting telecoms' "back doors"

Appendix 3

Fact sheet of the Economic and Trade Agreement (Phase One agreement) between the United States and China

Information on specific chapters of the Phase One agreement is provided below:

Intellectual Property. The Intellectual Property chapter addresses numerous longstanding concerns in the areas of trade secrets, pharmaceutical-related intellectual property, geographical indications, trademarks, and enforcement against pirated and counterfeit goods.

Technology Transfer. The Technology Transfer chapter sets out binding and enforceable obligations to address several of the unfair technology transfer practices of China that were identified in USTR's Section 301 investigation. For the first time in any trade agreement, China has agreed to end its long-standing practice of forcing or pressuring foreign companies to transfer their technology to Chinese companies as a condition for obtaining market access, administrative approvals, or receiving advantages from the government. China also commits to provide transparency, fairness, and due process in administrative proceedings and to have technology transfer and licensing take place on market terms. Separately, China further commits to refrain from directing or supporting outbound investments aimed at acquiring foreign technology pursuant to industrial plans that create distortion.

Agriculture. The Agriculture chapter addresses structural barriers to trade and will support a dramatic expansion of U.S. food, agriculture and seafood product exports, increasing American farm and fishery income, generating more rural economic activity, and promoting job growth. A multitude of non-tariff barriers to U.S. agriculture and seafood products are addressed, including for meat, poultry, seafood, rice, dairy, infant formula, horticultural products, animal feed and feed additives, pet food, and products of agriculture biotechnology.

Financial Services. The Financial Services chapter addresses a number of longstanding trade and investment barriers to U.S. providers of a wide range of financial services, including banking, insurance, securities, and credit rating services, among others. These barriers include foreign equity limitations and discriminatory regulatory requirements. Removal of these barriers should allow U.S. financial service providers to compete on a more level playing field and expand their services export offerings in the Chinese market.

Currency. The chapter on Macroeconomic Policies and Exchange Rate Matters includes policy and transparency commitments related to currency issues. The chapter addresses unfair currency practices by requiring high-standard commitments to refrain from competitive devaluations and targeting of exchange rates, while promoting transparency and providing mechanisms for accountability and enforcement. This approach will help reinforce macroeconomic and exchange rate stability and help ensure that China cannot use currency practices to unfairly compete against U.S. exporters.

Expanding Trade. The Expanding Trade chapter includes commitments from China to import various U.S. goods and services over the next two years in a total amount that exceeds China's annual level of imports for those goods and services in 2017 by no less than $200 billion. China's commitments cover a variety of U.S. manufactured goods, food, agricultural and seafood products, energy products, and services. China's increased imports of U.S. goods and services are expected to continue on this same trajectory for several years after 2021 and should contribute significantly to the rebalancing of the U.S.-China trade relationship.

Dispute Resolution. The Dispute Resolution chapter sets forth an arrangement to ensure the effective implementation of the agreement and to allow the parties to resolve disputes in a fair and expeditious manner. This arrangement creates regular bilateral consultations at both the principal level and the working level. It also establishes strong procedures for addressing disputes related to the agreement and allows each party to take proportionate responsive actions that it deems appropriate. The United States will vigilantly monitor China's progress in eliminating its unfair trade practices and implementing these obligations.

Source: The Office of the U.S. Trade Representative.

Bibliography

* Publications in Chinese.

Amiti, M., M. Dai, R. Feenstra and J. Romalis (2017) "How did China's WTO entry benefit US consumers?", *CEPR Discussion Paper 12076*.

Amiti, M., S. J. Redding and D. E. Weinstein (2019a) "The impact of the 2018 trade war on U.S. prices and welfare", *NBER Working Paper No. W25672*.

Amiti, M., S. J. Redding and D. E. Weinstein (2019b) "New China tariffs increase costs to U.S. households", *Federal Reserve Bank of New York*.

Autor, D. H., D. Dorn and G. H. Hanson (2013) "The China syndrome: Local labor market effects of import competition in the United States", *American Economic Review*, 103(6): 2121–2168.

Bagwell, K. and R. W. Staiger (1999) "An economic theory of GATT", *American Economic Review*, 89(1): 215.

Bhagwati, J. N. and T. N. Srinivasan (1976) "Optimal trade policy and compensation under endogenous uncertainty: The phenomenon of market disruption", *Journal of International Economics*, 6(4): 317–336.

Bhidé, A. V. and E. S. A. Phelps (2005) "A dynamic theory of China–U.S. trade: Making sense of the imbalances", *SSRN Paper No. 763284*.

Blonigen, B. A. (2002) "Tariff-jumping antidumping duties", *Journal of International Economics*, 57(1): 31–50.

Bown, C. P. (2019) "Phase one China deal: Steep tariffs are the new normal", *The Peterson Institute for International Economics*, December 19.

Brander, J. A. and B. J. Spencer (1985) "Export subsidies and international market share rivalry", *Journal of International Economics*, 18(1).

Broda, C., N. Limao and D. E. Weinstein (2008) "Optimal tariffs and market power: The evidence", *American Economic Review*, 98(5): 2032–2065.

Busch, M. L. (1999) *Trade Warriors: States, Firms, and Strategic Trade Policy in High-Technology Competition*, Cambridge: Cambridge University Press.

Cavallo, A., G. Gopinath, B. Neiman and J. Tang (2019) "Tariff passthrough at the border and at the store: Evidence from US trade policy", Department of Economics, Working Paper, Harvard University.

Cerutti E., G. Gopinath and A. Mohommad (2019) "The impact of China–US trade tensions", *IMF*, May 23.

Clausing, K. A. (2001) "Trade creation and trade diversion in the Canada-United States free trade agreement", *The Canadian Journal of Economics*, 34(3): 677–696.

Coleman, D. C. and C. Wilson (1958) "Profit and power: A study of England and the Dutch wars", *The Economic History Review*, 10(3).

Collie, D. R. (1991) "Export subsidies and countervailing tariffs", *Journal of International Economics*, 31: 309–324.

Collie, D. R. (1994) "Strategic trade policy and retaliation", *Japan & the World Economy*, 6(1): 75–88.

Conybeare A. C. John (1985) "Trade wars: A comparative study of Anglo-Hanse, Franco-Italian, and Hawley-Smoot conflicts", *World Politics*, 38(1): 147–172.

Conybeare A. C. John (1987) *Trade Wars: The Theory and Practice of International Commercial Rivalry*, New York: Columbia University Press.

Dixit, A. (1988) "Anti-dumping and countervailing duties under oligopoly", *European Economic Review*, 32(1): 55–68.

Dong, Y. and J. Whalley (2012) "Gains and losses from potential bilateral China–US trade retaliation", *Economic Modelling*, 29: 2226–2236.

Edgeworth, F. Y. (1894) "The theory of international values", *Economics Journal*, 4: 35–50.

Fajgelbaum, P. D., P. K. Goldberg, P. J. Kennedy and A. K. Khandelwal (2019) "The return to protectionism", *NBER Working Paper No. 25638*.

Feng, F., P. He and J. Han (2018) "How can free trade agreements ease the rule conflict of trade frictions", *China Industrial Economics*, 2018(10): 118–136.*

Gompert, D. C., A. S. Cavallas and C. L. Garafola (2016) "War with China: Thinking through the unthinkable", *RAND Corporation Report*.

Gorman, W. M. (1957) "Tariffs, retaliation, and the elasticity of demand for imports", *Review of Economic Studies*, 25: 33–162.

Gowa, J. (1989) "Rational hegemons, excludable goods, and small groups: An epitaph for hegemonic stability theory?", *World Politics*, 41(3): 307–324.

Greenland, A., M. Ion, J. Lopresti and P. K. Schott (2018) "Using equity market reactions to infer exposure to trade liberalization", Working Paper.

Gros, D. A. (1987) "A note on the optimal tariff, retaliation and the welfare loss from tariff wars in a framework with intra-industry trade", *Journal of International Economics*, 23(3–4): 0–367.

Grossman, G. M. and E. Helpman (1995) "Trade wars and trade talks", *Journal of Political Economy*, 103(4): 675–708.

Guo, M., L. Lu, L. Sheng and M. Yu. (2018) "The day after tomorrow: Evaluating the burden of Trump's trade war", *Asian Economic Papers*, 17(1): 101–120.

Handley, K. and N. Limão (2017) "Policy uncertainty, trade, and welfare: Theory and evidence for China and the United States", *American Economic Review*, 107(9): 2731–2783.

Handley, K. and N. Limão (2019) "The policy uncertainty aftershocks of trade wars and trade tensions", in M. A. Crowley (eds.) *Trade War: The Clash of Economic Systems Endangering Global Prosperity*, CEPR Press, May.

Hinton, R. W. K. (1959) *The Eastland Trade and the Commonweal in the Seventeenth Century*, Cambridge: Cambridge University Press.

Huang, P., J. Wang and X. Meng (2018) "Rebalance of economic globalization and trade frictions between China and the U.S.", *China Industrial Economics*, 2018(10): 156–174.*

Huang, Y., C. Lin, S. Liu and H. Tang (2019) "Trade networks and firm value: Evidence from the China–US trade war", *Social Science Electronic Publishing*.

Irwin, D. A. (2017) *Clashing over Commerce: A History of US Trade Policy*, Chicago: University of Chicago Press.

Johnson, H. G. (1954) "Optimum tariffs and retaliation", *Review of Economic Studies*, 21(2): 142–153.

Johnson, H. G. (1967) *International Trade and Economic Growth: Studies in Pure Theory*, Cambridge, MA: Harvard University Press.

Kennan, J. and R. Riezman (1988) "Do big countries win tariff wars?", *International Economic Review*, 29(1): 81–85.

Kindleberger, C. P. (1951) "Group behavior and international trade", *Journal of Political Economy*, 59(1): 30–46.

Krugman, P. R. (1986) *Strategic Trade Policy and the New International Economics*, Cambridge, MA: MIT Press.

Kuga, K. (1973) "Tariff retaliation and policy equilibrium", *Journal of International Economics*, 3(4): 351–366.

Li, C., C. He and C. Lin (2018) "Evaluating the effects of China's countermeasures to China–U.S. trade frictions", *China Industrial Economics*, 2018(10): 137–155.*

Liang, G. (2004) *New Competition: Foreign Direct Investment and Industrial Development in China*, Rotterdam: Erasmus Research Institute of Management, RSM.

Liang, G. (2017) *Chinese Economy 2040: The Changing Landscape of Globalization and a New Path of Development*, Beijing: Renmin University Press.

Lin, J. Y. and X. Wang (2018) "Trump economics and China–US trade imbalances", *Journal of Policy Modeling*, 40(3): 579–600.

Lu, Y., C. Lou, Y. Du and X. Tu (2019) "Analysis of the impact of Sino-US trade friction based on the tariff lists", *Journal of Finance and Economics*, 45(2): 59–72.*

Magee, C. S. P. (2008) "New measures of trade creation and trade diversion", *Journal of International Economics*, 75(2): 349–362.

Markusen, J. R. and R. M. Wigle (1989) "Nash equilibrium tariffs for the United States and Canada: The roles of country size, scale economies, and capital mobility", *Journal of Political Economy*, 97(2): 368–386.

Mayer, W. (1981) "Theoretical considerations on negotiated tariff adjustments", *Oxford Economic Papers*, 33(1): 135–153.

Motta, M. (1992) "Multinational firms and the tariff-jumping argument: A game theoretic analysis with some unconventional conclusions", *European Economic Review*, 36: 1557–1571.

Nicita, A. (2019) "Trade and trade diversion effects of United States tariffs on China", *UNCTAD Research Paper No. 37*, November.

Olson, M. and M. J. Bailey (1981) "Positive time preference", *Journal of Political Economy*, 89(1): 1–25.

Ossa, R. (2011) "A 'new trade' theory of GATT/WTO negotiations", *Journal of Political Economy*, 119(1): 122–152.

Ossa, R. (2014) "Trade wars and trade talks with data", *American Economic Review*, 104(12): 4104–4146.

Peltzman, S. (1976) "Toward a more general theory of economic regulation", *Journal of Law and Economics*, 19(2): 211–240.

Perroni, C. and J. Whalley (2000) "The new regionalism: Trade liberalization or insurance?", *Canadian Journal of Economics*, 33(1): 1–24.

Pierce, J. R. and P. K. Schott (2016) "The surprisingly swift decline of US manufacturing employment", *American Economic Review*, 106(7): 1632–1662.

Priestly, M. (1951) "Anglo-French trade and the unfavourable balance controversy, 1660–1685", *Economic History Review*, 4(1): 37–52.

Ratcliffe, B. (1978) "The tariff reform campaign in France, 1831–1836", *Journal of European Economic History*, 7, Spring: 61–138.

Ren, L. (2017) "Trump's trade policy and the US section 301 investigation against China", *Journal of International Trade*, 420(12): 155–167.*

Riezman, R. (1982) "Tariff retaliation from a strategic viewpoint", *Southern Economic Journal*, 48(3): 583–593.

Rosyadi S. A. and T. Widodo (2017) "Impacts of Donald Trump's tariff increase against China on global economy: Global trade analysis project (GTAP) model", *MPRA Paper No. 79493.*

Schlossstein, S. (1984) *Trade War: Greed, Power, and Industrial Policy on Opposite Sides of the Pacific*, New York: Congdon & Weed.

Smith, J. M. (1982) *Evolution and the Theory of Games*, Cambridge: Cambridge University Press, December.

Snyder, G. H. and P. Diesing (1977) *Conflict among Nations: Bargaining, Decision Making, and System Structure in International Crises*, Princeton: Princeton University Press.

Stigler, G. J. (1971) "The theory of economic regulation", *The Bell Journal of Economics and Management Science*, 2(1): 3–21.

Tower, E. (1975) "On the functional relationship between tariffs and welfare", *Atlantic Economic Journal*, 5(1): 65–66.

Viner, J. (1950) *The Customs Union Issue*, Carnegie Endowment for International Peace.

Whalley, J. (1958) *Trade Liberalization among Major World Trading Areas*, Cambridge, MA: MIT Press.

Wilson, C. (1957) *Profit and Power: A Study of England and the Dutch Wars*, London, New York and Toronto: Longmans, Green and Co.

Zhang, X., Y. Chen and F. Wu (2018) "May the export product quality upgrading reduce China's foreign trade frictions", *China Industrial Economics*, 2018(7): 43–61.*

Yang, F., W. Sun and Y. Cheng (2018) "Does technology catching-Up inspire Sino-U.S. trade friction", *China Industrial Economics*, 2018(10): 99–117.*

Yu, T. and B. Li (2004) "The cause of China–US trade frictions and policy solutions", *Management World*, 2004(9): 67–72.*

Index